OUTSPOKEN

MASTERING COMMUNICATION

AND

PUBLIC SPEAKING

MOHAMMAD ROOMI RATHER

〉〈〉〈〉〈

Woven Words Publishers OPC Pvt. Ltd.

Registered Office:

Vill: Raipur, P.O: Raipur Paschimbar,

Dist: Purba Midnapore, Pin: 721401,

West Bengal, India.

www.wovenwordspublishers.in

Email: editor@wovenwordspublishers.in

First published by Woven Words Publishers OPC Pvt. Ltd., 2018

Copyright© Bilal Ahmad Rather, 2018

NON-FICTION

IMPRINT: WOVEN WORDS NONFICTION

ISBN 13: 978-93-86897-24-4

ISBN 10: 9386897245

Price: $25/Rs. 220

Printed and bound in India

THANKS TO ....

I never thought of writing a book until less than a year ago when Allah (SWT) gave me this courage and strength to put all my experiences together at one place. So I would like to thank Allah – The Exalted One to make this easy for me. I don't want to miss this opportunity to go a little back in the time and recall all the incredible people I have had privilege to deal with during the time this book was in making.

It's my pleasure to thank Dr. Sanjeev Gupta (Dean) and Dr. Shameena Gupta (Director) – Academy of Technology and Management, Delhi for their inspiration and mentoring. It all started back in 2008 when you guys took me on board to professionalism.

Thanks to Akshat Srivastava, Anas Khan and Sameer Sharma (Candy) for their guidance. Being with you all in corporate world, I believe I was in the making and it was your presence that shaped me.

Thank you Dr. Ashfaq, Rizwana and Romana. Going down the memory lane, I relive all those magical and scary moments I spent with you guys. It has always been sensational living with you guys and being with you brought fore much learning.

Idrees, Owais, Nowreen and Basim - You guys are more than just colleagues. You have always been inspiring. I can never forget spending hours together discussing best ways to deliver the content. Writing a book would never have been possible without your support. Thank you so much for being there.

At this point in time I can't help but thank the Department of Management Studies, North Campus University of Kashmir for its great support in organizing all the seminars and workshops at the campus. This book has taken major inputs from the seminars and interactions I had with hundreds of students in the department and outside.

My special thanks to first batch of students I ever taught at Department of Management Studies, University of Kashmir North Campus – The batch of 2012. Guys, you all have been so loving and understanding. May you all succeed in your future endeavors.

Thank you Dr. Naseer Ahmad Rather, Tuba, Azra Mufti for dropping your busy schedule and reading and reviewing my broken paragraphs while they were being crafted.

Thanks to all my trusted colleagues especially Dr. Viqar-un-nisa, Dr. Ambreen Khursheed Wani, Dr. Altaf and Dr. Nusrat Ara for encouraging and appreciating my work.

Thanks to my family especially Nusrat, Parveena and Mudasir to bear my absence on the table. You guys were so longing for the completion of this book.

And finally, thanks to everyone who ever contributed to my learning, to hundreds of speakers I have observed and listened to in my life, to all my teachers I have ever been taught by since my childhood, to all those students whose presentations motivated me to write this book, to authors I have ever read and to anyone who deserved to be mentioned but was not, for the obvious reason of me being human.

To Mohammad (SAW), An Inspiration and Guide.
May Peace and Blessings Be Upon Him

And

To Ammi and Abha, for their never-ending love and support.
May Allah be pleased with you

And

To You - who left so soon. You wanted me to help the world through
every bit I can. Here I am, working on your dream. I don't know how, but
I believe you will get to know about my work and from over those skies,
you will smile at me!
Your absence is brutal, May you rest in Peace there.

FOREWORD

Communication skills and the art of public speaking might appear to be different from each other but in actuality are the two sides of the same coin: *Speaking*. More than the written word, the spoken word has changed the course of human history. Therefore, it is for good reasons that people have emphasized the importance of communication skills.

There is hardly anything more important than making yourself really good in the art of speaking and expressing yourself effectively and efficiently before public. Dr Kenneth McFarland in his book, *Eloquence in Public Speaking* (1963), while talking about the art of public speaking, lays more stress on the emotional component than on any methodology or technique. The key to a successful public speech is the way you keep the audience glued to yourself; they must really feel that they are getting what they had come for. The focus has therefore to be on the subject that you have chosen to speak on and care about it in the sense that it has impacted you and you really feel that it could benefit the listeners. Naturally, nobody would want to speak on any subject without making necessary preparation and planning. Ernest Hemingway, the world famous American novelist, once wrote that in order to write better, you must know ten words about the subject for every word that you write; otherwise it won't be considered true writing. In speaking, one must know more words for every word that we speak. If this doesn't happen the audience would feel that you don't know the subject at all. Therefore, all good public speakers who have had an impact on you, you must be sure, had given a lot of time to preparation and planning. Whether it is a ten minute lecture or a ten hour presentation, you have to take the audience into consideration and assess how to create the desired effect and impact on the listeners.

The present book discusses the various principles of the art of public speaking, starting with the 'Principle of Preparation and Practice'. It is not unusual for good speakers to spend a good amount of their time in preparing for a talk before they actually deliver it to the audience. You might feel that you are good at communicating and could deliver a talk without much of an effort. But, did the audience really feel at home when you were talking and did they feel that you were speaking on the subject? These questions are very crucial and must be borne in mind all the time whenever you intend to speak on any subject. On this count, the present book is a good addition to acquainting people with how to make an impact on the audience by following the well-established principles in the art of public speaking. Organization, facial expressions and body movements, voice quality, delivery and pace and eliminating the fear of rejection are some of the key principles in making yourself a good public speaker.

The book is divided into eight chapters, each chapter focusing on one of the principles in the art of public speaking. The last chapter entitled 'Principle of Conclusion' focuses on how to end one's speech. In this way, the present book becomes a kind of manual for the interested students and teachers who wish to make themselves good speakers. The Do's and Don'ts in speaking would enable the reader to mark his/her words and delivery so that what he/she says makes an impact on the listener/s. It is a well-organized treaty on the key elements in developing the art of public speaking, in general, and communication skills, in particular. The writer takes pains to make himself clear about the purpose of the book. He says, "Undoubtedly, this book is about communication and public speaking. However, not just to tell you how to speak before big crowds and send across your message. Rather, it's to tell you how to connect with people heart-to-heart and mind-to-mind." This is an important statement somewhat similar to Dr McFarland's who has talked about the emotional aspect of the public speaking.

The book is based on personal experiences of the writer, as a student and teacher, for over a decade. Naturally, the book has to be taken as the first hand information on why our students, in general, and many teachers, in particular, fail to deliver effective lectures or speeches. His 'Secret Essentials' are therefore a way forward to making students and teachers good speakers without necessarily *teaching* these *essentials* in the classroom. Can we really teach the art of public speaking? The answer could be given both in negative and positive. Communication is primarily *fluency*, an activity that needs to be developed by practice; it comes with the habit of speaking more and more and taking care of mistakes on your own. Therefore, there can't be any *teaching* per se in *fluency*. However, the classroom can become the initial platform for training students to speak under the guidance of a well-trained teacher and before an audience. After all, it is the teacher who makes more impact on the students than anybody else. For building their self-confidence, the students can be asked to prepare smaller speeches which can be assessed and evaluated by their peers in the class. This could go a long way in preparing students for their future events and for speaking before huge gatherings.

Teachers and students who deal with communications skills and/or public speaking as part the syllabus should benefit from the book to the extent that it leads them through the key elements in the art of public speaking. However, how it is used in the classroom can be evaluated only once the book goes into the hands of practicing teachers and their students. In the present day global scenario, the importance of speaking can hardly be ignored; the more skillful you are, the better impact you can have on the listeners. Therefore, the present book should evoke a good interest in both teachers and students.

Professor Mohammad Aslam
Formerly, Head, Department of English
Dean, School of Languages and
Director, Research and Development
Central University of Kashmir

"If all my possessions were taken from me with one exception, I would hope to keep my power of communication – for by it I would regain all the rest"

Woody Allen

CONTENTS

PREFACE

You might be sitting out there wondering what this book is going to be all about. And those wild guesses considering the title of the book may as well be helping with the curiosity. Well, let me just keep the suspense for a while and tell you that this book is not what you think it is about. In part, it may be! But for the most part, you are certainly going to find it different.

We all believe that communication skills are very much critical to how effective we could be in our professional and personal lives. And most of the times when we think of communication, we think of speaking with special focus on content of our message. However, little do we realize that sometimes we mean a lot without even saying a word, we break hearts worth billions by just turning our face away and we make ever lasting relationships by just passing a smile. If it was all about speaking, world would leave no space for those gifted fellows who can't speak or who can't hear, right? But guess what, these people live with us. They understand everything about us and so do we about them. I would rather say, they communicate with us. So to prove a point, communication is not just speaking, it's something beyond. Communication is about emotions, love, connection – I believe it's about conduct.

Undoubtedly, this book is about communication and public speaking. However, not just to tell you how to speak before big crowds and send across your message. Rather it's to tell you how to connect with people heart-to-heart and mind-to-mind. It is to share with you some secrets about winning listener's heart and then keeping it for a while. It's about knowing how to leave people wanting more.

During my decade long observation right from the start of my MBA program in 2008, I have met people from diverse backgrounds either as a student, classmate, subordinate, colleague, panelist, teacher and mentor or very recently as a communications trainer. Something that I could feel about most of them, and possibly something that motivates me to write this book is that "They need help with communication". Most of them would no wonder do great in their technical field and mechanics but would fail big time when it comes to connecting with people. I have seen management graduates doing wonders in understanding managerial concepts, but when it comes to people skills – the very essence of being a management graduate, they struggle.

Participating in seminars and having organized few of them, I met many students, teachers and other professionals one-on-one and in groups, trying to help them overcome the stage fear, public appearances and rescue them of their communication problems. That however didn't seem to be enough. Had I been still doing that, I couldn't have reached out to you. So it seemed more appealing to pen down these secrets to effective communication to make sure it helps even those I couldn't otherwise reach out to.

One may keep on just wondering, asking what is it these speakers do that I don't and end up doing nothing but longing to be like them. Or one may dig a little deeper and actually figure out what these great speakers do and be one of them. Yes, that's where I break the suspense, this is what my book is all about – to dig a little deeper and know what makes some people so much effective that even after hours of speaking people still want to listen to them. And then there is handsome guy with convincing looks and strong academic and professional background who can't even engage people for 10 minutes. You see nothing huge behind this magnificent difference between them, but just a few principles that this former buddy knowingly or unknowingly goes by, that prove him as an effective speaker.

These principles which I would like to call the "Secret Essentials" are everything behind an effective speaker. To make it easy for you to understand these principles and get the most out of them, I have discussed them in separate chapters of the book. Given to the precise content and small size of the book, I know some bookworms can finish it in just one sitting. But that won't serve the purpose. I don't want this book be just another read for you. To see a real change in your communication skills, I suggest a scheme of reading this book in parts, not in just one sitting. The reader should ponder on the chapter details, note down the suggestions made and compare his existing state of communication with the dimension that's being discussed. Once you know the secret, there is no point in waiting - go on and give it a place in your professional or academic life and start applying it right away.

I believe this book shall serve great inputs to teachers of any level, especially the ones at higher education level who face mature and thinking audience. I don't promise to give you some magic wand, but certainly some practical things to do that shall help you engage your students beyond the traditional 45-minute Indian class.

I am directing this book to one and all - especially those who need to do the formal speaking of some kind on daily basis – like Teachers, trainers, instructors, students and sales executives. The principles discussed herein are universal and tested over time. They have worked for me as an employee, as teacher, as instructor, as mentor and above all – as human. I believe they can work for anyone who needs to get his message across, who needs to convince people, face the audience, speak across and communicate. I believe they can certainly work for you.

So get ready. Being effective is just a read away . . . . Happy Reading!

Yours Effectively
Mohammad Roomi Rather

PRINCIPLE OF PREPRATION AND PRACTICE

Being an effective speaker is not a spontaneous process. It takes thousands of hours of preparation and practice overcoming minor and eventually the major challenges as you move along. The great speakers we know about did not become so overnight. They all started at some point as amateurs like all of us, and as they moved along this continuum of practice they helped themselves overcome the problems like anxiety, nervousness, fear of audience and like. Think of an athlete who we see performing for just 15 minutes in Olympics. How many of us do think about the fact that it takes this same athlete prepare and practice consistently for 15 years before he actually gets to perform in Olympics? Most of us are driven by results and achievements and we are highly receptive to this, but only few of us are ready for the struggle and effort that forms the base of this achievement. It goes the same way about communication and public speaking. If we want to learn communicating, we have to start communicating.

If you want to be an athlete, start running
If you want to be a speaker, start speaking

Practice makes a man perfect, that's what all of us have been hearing since childhood. This saying however doesn't hold good when it comes to communicating. You can never be a perfect speaker, nobody has ever been and no one tries to be. All you have to strive for is to be an **effective speaker**. You may as well take speaking and communication for granted because all of us do speak and communicate somehow, somewhere to some extent on daily basis. However, when your performance, prosperity, grades as a student and stakes as an employee or teacher are linked to it, you have something to think about.

Now, one may think how do I practice communicating? And while you have this question in mind, I can say this with utter assurance that most of us are thinking about speaking – which forms just a part of communicating. Our purpose here is not to just learn how to be a great speaker, rather how to be an effective communicator – someone who at times doesn't even say a word and still means a lot. So to answer this question – How do I practice? I suggest going as follows.

Find Yourself: When I started learning communication, I would always find my mentors saying, you need a learning environment where everyone and everything around you helps you towards the objective of being an effective speaker. If for instance you need to learn how to speak a language, you need to be around people who would speak that language, read books to know the basics of that language and may be watch movies and dramas in that language. All that being regarded high; I believe there is something that comes way before looking for environment and that is **Your Own Self**.

Now what do I mean by saying find yourself. A few years back, one of my students approached me after a communication class. He was possibly inspired by the session we had and asked straight away, "Sir, I can speak a little English, but I want to speak it fluently. How can I get there?" My answer was too short for him to understand. I replied, "Think in English". The next thing was quite expected, "Sir, how do I think in English?" I went on explaining of which I will give you a fair idea here. Humans do a lot of thinking and if we just analyze our thinking it's nothing but speaking to our own self. We normally speak to ourselves in native languages, the language that we readily understand and interpret. Linguistically speaking, we first understand and interpret the meaning of a language and then start speaking it, be it native or otherwise. Now if someone starts thinking in English, that means understands and interprets its meaning, he can certainly speak it. This doesn't need you any environment or situation. It needs you to speak to your own self. This is the biggest secret to languages. You only master a language when you are able to think in that language.

Easy said than done, we can't reach this level of thinking all at once. It takes consistent efforts over longer periods. Go ahead and try narrating a story to your own self, share the details of shopping experience you had today, encourage yourself to do good, speak to yourself about this new teacher or this book, introspect and give yourself grades based upon your level of communication - all this be done in the language you want to master.

Socialize: Now that you have found yourself and you like to interact with your inner partner, there is this desperate need to know how well you are doing. This part is about turning to people outside. You have to start speaking, try your gestures and body language before people because it's ultimately they who will make your audience. It's more like test marketing your communication skills and knowing where and how much you need to work on them.

It gets a bit harder in beginning and one may just feel insecure, anxious and worried about what others think. But this is how the journey begins.

It is more like travelling to a destination that's too far and you don't see it yet. How much time it is going to take to get there will depend on how well you go on the way. On this journey you will certainly find people of your kind who know nothing more than you, they are just travelling along. These people will make you little comfortable because with them you realize that you are not alone. However, on the same journey you will find people who have travelled before this way and have been to the place where you are heading. They are the ones you need to look out for and spend time with. If you are not blessed enough to be with them, at least watch them moving on this way, observe every step they take. If possible, copy them and work on their advice. There is also the third category of people walking along, possibly the one of great importance to you. They are the people who have never travelled to the destination either, but know a lot more about this journey from their relatives, friends or mentors who have been here before. They are the ones you need more. Make up with them and join hands, for this is the group that you can benefit the most from. They won't expect you to know much because you never travelled before and in turn given to what they know from their friends and relatives, they will have so much to offer.

Learning Orientation: Be positive and optimistic about your goal of being an effective communicator. This would require you looking for opportunities where you can practice your skills and acquire new ones. As a student go regularly to the classes where a teacher engages his students more and gives them fair opportunity to speak out and try their skills. Be the first one to register for participation in a guest lecture, conference, seminar, debates and other non-academic activities. These are the platforms where you can watch others communicating and take tremendous inputs for your practice. Out of many takeaways, the ones you should carefully observe as beginner are preparation, delivery, gestures, body language, sound pitch, pronunciation and audience engagement.

As learners, we should never lose the opportunity of communicating, be it spontaneous or planned. Spontaneously, it could be your boss asking you to explain the departmental profile to the newly joined employees or your teacher asking you to stand up and explain a concept. And the planned opportunity could be your key note speech in a conference next week or your classroom presentation scheduled for this weekend.

Visualize: The principle of visualization works perfectly good in communication. Winners in all aspects of life have one thing in common, they practice visualization. As the saying goes:

"What you visualize is what you materialize".

Visualization serves as a great practice. Whatever your goal may be, you should not just think of it, but feel it happening. Every business has a vision which is nothing but visualization of its future. Just like an athlete closes his eyes and imagines winning a run by split second, a salesman envisions closing a deal, a soccer player visualizes conceding a goal – you should visualize yourself delivering an effective presentation, giving a fabulous talk and a momentous speech.

There are two things that take us forward in our life – **Skill** and **Will**. Visualization helps you generate will, which in turn drives you towards skill. It intensifies your desire and makes you enthusiastic towards your goal. Will prevails in a situation where skill fails.

The great boxing icon Mohammad Ali once described it in an apt way. He said that in a boxing ring, I fight my opponent with my boxing skill. Many times he would knock me down and I would have to sum up my strength and rise again. But this rising was not because of my skill, which was just beaten by my opponent – I would rise because of my will to bounce back, to knock him down - The will to be a winner.

All that being said, will needs to be supported by skill. Else your visualization would just be a day dreaming. We will discuss the skill part in subsequent chapters of the book. For now, we will understand visualization in depth to make sure it works to our benefit.

How Does Visualization Help?
A human brain is like a pattern detecting machine and visualization is about detecting patterns. So when you visualize yourself standing before huge audience in a hall, your brain starts developing patterns envisioning hall settings. That's why it is much recommended for beginners to have a glimpse of an empty hall and its settings before actually hitting it when it is gem pact. It helps overcome anxiety and nervousness to a great extent in the sense that part of the suspense is over when you know where and

in what pattern your audience would be sitting. You can expect the number of people you would be facing and their nearness to the stage. Now this might as well be possible that you don't get to have a glimpse of the hall settings before you hit the stage – which happens by the way very often when you are in speaking business. In such a case it is recommended that while you walk to the stage, you should not start right away with your speech. It is better to take a moment and look around. Take a deep breath and feel relaxed. In this time your brain will to a major extent develop all the patterns it did earlier when you had a glimpse of the stage.

In a typical college of Indian settings students would be seated in a class a few minutes earlier than when a teacher steps in. In this time that may vary from 5-7 minutes, students would get ready for the lecture or discussion, turn on the projector, adjust their seats and many would indulge in gossips and fun. Now imagine a student using this time to visualize his presentation. If he is a beginner and has never faced the audience before, this is the great opportunity for him to overcome his nervousness and suspense. He can slowly move to the podium, stand there for a while and know the hall settings and the audience he would be facing.

Visualization helps us get ready to face what's coming by preparing our minds. It is thinking and preparing about our performance well in advance. And ultimately, what we think about is what we bring about.

If we visualize consistently, our minds become used to the prospect of public speaking that helps to conquer the feelings of anxiety.

An effective teacher visualizes his delivery inside the class. A significant part of his preparation involves visualizing quoting a fine example to students, proving a point, using a particular gesture and facial expression to convey the importance of a statement he makes. Based upon the complexity of the facts and figures he has to present, he visualizes where he needs to take a pause or keep the flow and the points he may have to repeat to the audience. An effective teacher envisions his class giving him a nod of understanding.

There is More to Preparation

I was in a meeting once with the head of one of the institutions I worked with. He was a professor of eminence with more than 3 decades of experience in higher education. While advising his newly joined colleagues he made a point of sheer importance. He said, "Don't ever go the class unless you are fully prepared. It takes thousand classes for a teacher to build a reputation and a single moment to unpreparedness to break it down. You are teaching millenials and they are mature, informed and won't take even a shred of a second to realize what you are doing in a class".

While many of you, as did many of my colleagues sitting in that meeting, think that preparation is about developing an understanding of the concept, assembling facts and figures from credible sources and getting ready to answer the questions your students might ask, I believe there is lot more to it. A teacher should first of all get in the mood to teach, which besides developing a concept understanding needs you to get over your personal engagements. We are all human beings and things do happen in our personal and social life that bring us down and this certainly reflects from our professional conduct. An effective teacher keeps his personal side aside, sums up his energy and brings that charisma on his face. He gets himself ready mentally and physically to rock and roll – this is what I call as **"getting in the mood"**. The next thing a teacher has to do is to prepare for his delivery. The question is not just about what to say and what to present, it is also about how to say and how to present. In my short academic career I have noticed many teachers with doctorate in their subjects and having qualified highly competitive exams to get into the academic profession fail miserably inside the class. Looking at the flip side I have as well seen people who just graduated and are yet to develop enough knowledge base required to be an effective teacher doing fair enough. The difference is in the **how** part of the class, not **what** part of it.

A teacher concentrating on what to teach would be driven by information part of his session and would miss on student engagement. However a teacher considering how to teach makes information just a part of his session, but delivers it in a way that students take it lively and would never miss. The following saying sums up it all.

Tell me and I forget
Teach me and I remember
Engage me and I learn

"What" makes you a good narrator and the "How"– an effective Communicator.

Design Your Delivery

A speaking professional and an effective presenter would always prepare a design for his speech. He knows what to say and when to say it. There are many elements to this design and all of them have to be perfectly placed at desired stages of your speech. Designing involves giving a fine structure to your presentation or speech so that you know what comes first and what comes after it. An effective communicator for instance uses jokes as one of the elements of his speech. He doesn't use a joke just to make his audience laugh, but this joke should rather relate to the message he is trying to deliver and help audience connect to the purpose the speaker is using the joke for.

While we design our speech or presentation, the original concept or message and fact and figures will make only part of it. There are many other elements we need to incorporate in it to make sure our audience remains engaged throughout.

Quotes/Facts: They make up an important part of your speech by helping you underpin your credibility. Quotes are to be used in general nonacademic, self-help or motivational speeches. It helps your audience believe in your statements by connecting your opinion with that of someone who has a known standing. And the facts are for academic and other statistics based speeches like that of teachers in his class. Facts enhance the credibility of a teacher and are the primary takeaways for students. A teacher for the authenticity of the information has to mention the source of the facts in his presentation as well.

Examples: The next important element of your speech design would be the real world examples. They help you turn your abstract statement into something concrete. Delivering a speech without examples is actually more work for your audience in the sense that they will have to think more to understand your message. And as a speaker you don't want your audience to be lost in thinking while you have moved on to say something else, do you? An effective speaker takes his audience along and makes them listen and follow every single statement he makes. This goal is achieved by quoting examples. Examples lead to quick understanding and hence audience doesn't get lost.

Jokes: We use jokes as another element of our speech design. Their primary purpose is to light up the audience's mood and keep their attention. However unless you are a comedian, which for sure most of you won't be, you should never use a joke for the sole purpose of making an audience laugh. Every single funny remark we make, we should always try to connect it to some factual piece of information.

For example, I was once discussing the role of culture in strategy formulation of a global restaurant chain, say McDonald's, in my class. While we were pointing out the food habits of people of different nations as in them being vegetarian and non-vegetarian, I had to say – We in Kashmir are All-tarians but pigitarians!, which meant we eat almost everything but pigs. This by the way is a fact that everyone understood with a little laugh on the face.

The designing of your speech should as well be the design of your delivery. That means writing should go hand in hand with practice. We should read out our sentences aloud immediately after we write them down just to see what they sound like when spoken. Quite often they sound different than what we imagined they would sound like. Ultimately we may need to rearrange our words, use a different tone or just another pitch.

So while preparing for your session, look for relevant examples, quotes and jokes and find a place for them in your speech to make sure they add beauty to your delivery.

Now if you have really understood the principle of preparation and practice well, I believe you are ready to move on to the next level of hitting the stage and know how to introduce yourself and get started.

PRINCIPLE OF INTRODUCTION

The first impression is the last impression – this saying works well with communication. The concept of primacy does have its effect as does the recency. You are not always going to interact with an amateur audience who have never been to any professional session before and don't know what effective speakers look like. In fact such audience doesn't exist anymore. We all have been exposed to some kind of formal speaking sessions at different age groups. A typical morning assembly session of Indian schools, weekly and monthly guest speech by the head of the managing body of your school, religious sermons in mosques, churches and temples, formal debates and conferences at secondary and senior secondary levels and the lecture and presentation sessions at college and university level – all of these sessions make us a well learned audience over time and we can figure out the cool and not-so-cool speakers. So whenever we start our presentation or delivery session, we need to be off to a bursting and booming start. As audience it doesn't take us more than 10 minutes to realize how effective this session is going to be. So the control on first few moments helps us take our audience along. If they are with you in the beginning, they will for the most part be with you in the end. As the saying goes;

"Be with them when you take off, they will be with you in the landing".

People don't have time and they don't come to listen to a speaker. They rather come for their own interests and need to know what's in there in your speech for them. They need to know why is this session worth one or two hours of their time and how can they can benefit from it. So as a speaker you need to prove the importance of the session and clear the air around few questions like what would they learn from it? And how is it going to benefit them? This is what makes the introduction part worth preparing.

Now, one may ask what we have to do for an effective an enthusiastic start. And the answer to this question lies in understanding the following discussion.

24

Thank Your Audience and the Organizers: As a speaker you have to be courteous and thank everyone who made this event possible. You can start right away by thanking your listeners for making it to the venue and organizers for having you. Don't forget to refer to the person who introduced you, thank him for his kind introduction. You can also refer to a few senior people in the organizing body or audience if you happen to know any. This makes you look courteous before audience and also compliments those you have mentioned.

Being done with Thanksgiving! Now is the time to kick off with a bang.

Bringing Minds Together: An effective speaker is a highly rational person. He understands that his audience comes from various spheres of life and they are not on the same page while sitting in one common hall. Frequently, most of them may not have left their home and came directly for this session. They may just be coming from listening to another presentation on an altogether different topic, after having finished their meeting with a client or an argument with their boss, after school or a court hearing. They may also have come to escape from something else or meet with another attendee. Cutting it short, the audience would never be equally ready for your session given to the state of affairs they have just left. As an effective speaker it's your job to start in a way so that all of them come to one single focus – You. You have to begin in a way that they forget where they came from and make them feel this is what they were looking for. That means to assemble all the shattered minds to one common platform and this is what I call – Bringing minds together. We can do this in many ways and every different speaker may have his own ways of doing this. However, try the following – they are proven and tested.

Start with a wow question: We see majority of speakers starting their session with their own introduction. It is no wrong to start so, however not so effective. The common sense says whenever we see someone whom we have never seen before, speaking, the first question striking our mind is – who is this guy? So when you start away with who you are, you are doing nothing creative for audience to bring their minds together because that's what they expected you to do. You failed to break the inertia of their mind and it's no great for you as speaker. What we can do as an alternative is to start with a question that makes them think for a while, a question that people rarely know the answer of.

For instance, in a recent session with a class of my students I started off with a question – Is there anyone sitting in the hall who can tell me how many times has sun approximately risen so far? One of the students from the middle row stood up and replied, Sir, the earth is believed to be 4.5 billion years old and in that sense sun must have risen 4.5 billion times so far. Then I asked, is there anyone else who agrees with this gentleman? Yes, half of the class. Then someone from rest half of the class stood up, Sir, If not 4.5 billion years exactly, but yes it must be billions of years. A lady supporting this answer in the first row said Sir, Sun rises every day, and as many days this earth has witnessed, that many times the sun has risen. Everyone seemed to be satisfied and I took a pause. While everyone was looking at me and waiting for me to give my nod for this answer, I said no. The sun has risen only once since the dawn of the universe. I could see everyone shocked in the class except a couple of them from science background who knew what I mean. I had to explain that sun never rises and it never sets. It is always there. It's rising and setting is the phenomenon related to rotation of earth. When it sets in India, it rises in America. It's there and will never set and never rise again.

I could sense my question becoming a wow question.....!

This is how a wow question can snatch the audience attention and make them forget everything else they have left behind. It activates and charges them up. It forces them to focus on you and then you can set the boat sailing.

Share a Fact: It's also wise to start with a fact but only if it has to do with your subject. You don't want to look like a fool by quoting some irrelevant fact like 'it saves Rs.5000 per year on car mileage by maintaining adequate tire pressure' when you are going to speak about global poverty. Do you? It's good to talk about great ideas in abstract terms, but it becomes real when we support it by numbers and facts. Quoting a fact sets the tone for the discussion to come and a speaker has to relate this fact to his subject after he is done with the introduction.

Sharing a statistics based fact can help us in tremendous ways as speaker. It has an emotional impact that helps audience connect to you right from the very beginning. For example, you can quote the percentage of kids in your city who won't have enough to fill their stomach this holiday season, if your subject is poverty. It makes you credible in the sense that audience gets to know how well you have researched your topic and how hard you have worked for your audience. The credibility is more when you quote the facts from authentic sources like World Health

26

Organization. Using statistics based fact has a lasting effect, so your audience will remember you long after the session is over.

Kick off with a Joke: Another great practice to have a focused audience is to start off with a joke. There is no better antidote to overcome entropy of people's minds than something that makes them smile. In a formal setting we don't want people to laugh out their lungs, but certainly something that warms them up and takes you an inch closer to their mind. So a joke has to be of modest kind where you don't expect a full blown laughter, but just a kind of teaser to bring everyone to your table. A speaker has to be careful about not to make a joke at the expense of his audience or the event organizing company or someone who introduced you. Unless you are a standup comedian such things are to be avoided. However, a joke at the expense of your own self works really well. For instance, a joke like this one may work fairly well.

"Thank you for coming here, I will make sure you regret coming to this session".

However such jokes shall be made by a comparatively confident speaker who knows his content and has been in speaking business for a while. For a beginner who is not sure how this presentation is going to work, a joke like this one would work nice.

"Before leaving for the talk my wife said to me: 'Don't try to be too intellectual and charming, just be yourself"

These are just some ideas that may work in one setting or another. Apparently, a joke that you come up yourself with is going to do better. It would have to do with the context and the situation. The more a joke is appropriate to the situation, better it is going to work.

Compliment the Audience: A Speaker may as well begin by complimenting his listeners with sincerity and respect. Tell them how honorable it is for you to be before them and prove to them how important they are. When I interact with students of junior semesters I try to make them realize their importance by connecting their general abilities and talents with the requirements of the system they are in. For a particular audience you may have to do a little of research to know about them. This will help in customizing your compliments for them. The biggest compliment your audience can have from you is a smile. So smile as if you are really glad to see them.

27

To further make them feel good, you could say something like:
"It's my immense pleasure to be here with you today. You are really great people, given to what you all can do for this society and world. I am very much hopeful that this is going to be one of the best sessions I have ever had".

Start with Positivity and Hope: Start your session by telling your audience how they are going to like every moment you spend with them. Tell them, "I am going to give you some great insights into the subject that you possibly might not have been through before". Give them hope that this session is going to change their thinking and behavior, if not life. As a speaker, your purpose would always be to inspire people for something they never tried before. So when you speak purposely to inspire, you are giving them some kind of hope.

As a communications trainer I have seen people who are quiet averse to face public, especially in formal settings. These people have many genuine reasons to be so just like anyone else in the world. Nervousness, forgetfulness, facing questions, lack of confidence and language are just a few to mention. Interacting with these people is always going to be something special and driven by motivation. What these people mostly need is hope and inspiration from speaker.

To inspire and give them hope, I often tell them that, *"All the speakers you watch on TED talks or elsewhere were not like that from the start. They were just like you and me, nervous and anxious about speaking. But they realized there weaknesses, worked on them one by one till they mastered them all. This didn't happen all at once, it took them years to accomplish what you see in them now. They didn't give up until they really could do it.*
The bottom line is, if anyone in the world has done it, you can do it as well. Feel good knowing that you are not alone when it comes to stage fear, there are 85% people globally who feel the same. And one author even says that rest 15% are lying.
So all you need to do is start today and start from little things, a day will come when you will have a say and the world will have to listen".

Start with a Story: One of the finest ways you can kick off your session with is to start with a story. Quoting Brain Tracy, "Some of the most powerful words that grab the complete attention of the audience are, *"Once upon a time..."* When you say this, people would immediately become quiet and settle down. Stories help you create the hook right from the beginning. All you need to make sure is that your story reflects the message you are going to deliver.

A technique that can work even better is to start with a story and not finish it. Keep the suspense and let them know they will get to know the rest very soon. This half-told story works fine as concluding technique as well. When you are finishing your session, you can tie the opening and closing of your speech by sharing with your audience the other half of the story. This is called "rounding off" and helps you in closing with bang. For instance, if I am in a session that inspires people for communicating, I can start like this:

"Being an effective communicator is all about practice and consistency. A few years ago, there was this lady namely **Hafsa**, she had recently joined the MBA program and was called for her first ever presentation. When she went to podium I could literally see her shivering and dropping the papers. All she could do for those 40 seconds she managed to hang on there was to break down and cry. She then came to me for the obvious reason of knowing what to do. I spoke to her and shared some simple communication principles with her. I told her just to work on them and let me know about your progress. They were the same principles that I am going to discuss with you today. Be with me, I will update you about her current status."

Introduction

Now, when you have broken the ice and are off to great start, it's time to introduce your self to the audience. Effective introductions generally involve three essential elements and we call this **Speaker-Subject-Audience (SSA)** principle.

Speaker: A speaker should first introduce himself keeping in mind that he doesn't alienate the audience while speaking about his achievements. I would recommend not speaking much about your accomplishments at this stage. They do matter and audience needs to know the person speaking is worth listening to, but it often detaches the audience from speaker in the sense that are not able to relate to the person and consider him not being one of them. An MBA graduate who has just passed out from college won't be able to relate himself to Bill Gates or Jeff Bezos. These big guns have decades of experience, tones of capital and tremendous influence. This graduate who has nothing but his academic degree would possibly relate himself better with a recent Indian startup by an average student who also finished his MBA a year ago. People don't want to listen to someone who is very much perfect and above par; they would rather listen to someone who they can relate with.

So while introducing, care should be taken to look real and make everyone comfortable by presenting yourself as being one of them. The achievements are to be spoken about throughout the session at exact places to help reinforce your message. Backing your message by some achievement makes it credible and serves as an inspiration to people.

Subject: In the next part, speaker tries to answer the question – why are we here? That's to introduce his subject. The audience is very curious to know few things in the beginning. One of them is to know what this session is all about. So as a speaker you need to introduce the subject keeping in mind your introduction answers the WIIFM question as well. This is a complementary question that generally goes with the former one. It is the question of audience interest – **W**hat **I**s in **I**t **F**or **M**e?

People are running short of time and 24 hours seems too little for 21st century. Unless you give them strong reason for being there and show them how important this session is for them, they would hardly be ready to listen to you. People live by a perfect business mood and before they invest their time, money and effort anywhere they would analyze the returns. So as a transaction they want something back for their time. This session is about answering a few questions before they are even asked – Why is this session important, how is it going to benefit the audience and how it can help them in future. Your introduction to the subject should clearly reflect your knowledge of the subject that would come from your preparation.

Audience: The first two parts of the SSA principle have to be designed in conformity with this last part. Doesn't matter how hard you try to introduce yourself or your subject, it's the audience that has to find it interesting. Besides, everyone wants to be praised and spoken about, so you should never forget to make a statement about the people sitting in the hall. A speaker has to show some courtesy and be grateful to his audience for taking time to come to the session. It obviously wouldn't have been possible without them being there.

Further, people are never comfortable sitting next to strangers and you would quite often have an audience coming from different places and backgrounds knowing nothing about the fellow guys sitting next to them. A speaker has to give an attempt and make people comfortable by introducing them to one another. This for the most part would require you to know some details about the audience before you hit the stage. It is about giving value and engaging them mentally from the very beginning, and if you think it's worthwhile for you as a speaker, we better give it some time researching it.

The crux of the SSA principle is asking yourself where do I want to take my audience and if my speech works, what do people believe in after it is done. We have to know the answer to this question before we design our introduction. A speaker has a goal - any statement or word that helps attaining that goal can stay and anything that doesn't add to the case, gets cut.

PRINCIPLE OF ENGAGEMENT

We have all been through our share of boring presentations and speaking session where we are forced to listen to the content that's being delivered, not discussed with us. According to a "Meetings in America" study conducted by MCI, an impressive 39 percent of respondents confessed to falling asleep at some point during business meetings and presentations. As a speaker it would be unnerving to be looking at a sea of faces that look like they would rather be somewhere else. The burden of engagement would always lie on your shoulder as a speaker and you can only hope for dynamic and engaged crowd whom you find interacting. But this won't come by accident. It requires you to craft, frame and present your message in a way that involves your audience early and often. It is a challenge for any public speaker to connect to the people sitting in a hall. And to win over this challenge we can't treat our presentation just as a performance and audience as mere spectators. A speaker has to break the imaginary wall that keeps the audience from becoming part of his action. This could be done by making your session an interaction rather than a lecture.

A study conducted by Indiana University reveals that an average adult listens effectively for only about 15-20 minutes, and then he begins to wander. Now for us, knowing that our session is going to last for an hour or a typical 45 minute class of Indian education settings would obviously require us to do more. A speaker can make great use of this study. Knowing that a person can't focus for more than 15 minutes, we can change things and interrupt the pattern of our speech after every 15 minutes. This could be done by asking a provocative question, incorporating a physical activity, offer a humorous anecdote or something situational that you believe breaks the rhythm of your speech. This helps speaker buy himself more time and overcome the 15 minutes threshold of a person's focus.

In this chapter we would discuss some effective and tested techniques to keep our audience engaged throughout and leave them wanting more. There is nothing more soothing for a speaker than hearing someone from his audience say, "I wish he could speak for a little longer".

Speak to Serve: At the very outset, clear your aim and objectives and let people know why you are there. They have to know what you can do for them and what is it that they can leave with. After all, the objective is to benefit the audience through teaching, motivation or entertainment, not you. This for a twist is certainly going to work for you as well. When you take focus off of yourself and shift it to the audience, much of the fear and nervousness is gone. Once you know what you have to do for them, you have the purpose. Now you can color your delivery accordingly and your voice, gestures and body language become the clear evidences for your audience to know the efforts you put to help them learn something. And there is no better motivator for a person to listen effectively than a speaker putting efforts for him.

We have to spell out clearly and equivocally the benefits we are providing to those giving us time and attention. The audience has to feel valued and know the speaker is there for them and this would be the beginning of their engagement.

Create a Hook from the Start: As they say, First impression is the last impression and that we never get the second chance to create the first impression. So the first few minutes are to be used to create this impression. We can do this by making a provocative statement, asking a thought provoking question or relevant anecdote that sets up the topic we are going to discuss. More important, we can ask a question of great interest that we don't answer right away and the answer lies in the presentation. We can build suspense in audience by withholding some information or facts about the subject to hook them along till finish.

There was this economist who was invited for a guest lecture at our institution. He had to speak to newly joined students most of whom didn't have the economics background. The topic for discussion was Inflation and Money Supply. I found him an effective communicator in a way that he really hooked up the class right from the beginning. He started with a question that buzzes around every beginner's mind, even that of a layman. He asked, "Why doesn't central bank print enough currency for all citizens of a country to eradicate poverty?" Knowing nothing about the inflation and its effects, this seemed to be the viable option for newly joined students and everyone wanted to know why we don't print enough money. The economist didn't answer the question and hooked them up by saying, "By the end of this session you all should be in a position to answer this question yourself".

I reckon the speaker knew his audience, the situation and knew his subject. He kicked off differently and engaged them throughout. Everyone listened attentively and for the most part, did answer the question at last.

Make it a Conversation: Any speaking session or presentation has to be a dialogue, rather than a monologue. Although much of the talking has to be done by the speaker, audience has to come in frequently if we want them to be engaged. Soliciting feedback, asking questions and checking in at various intervals to confirm understanding are some ways to bring the audience in. People will pay attention if they know they will have to participate at some point. Participation doesn't mean their involvement with speaker only, but an opportunity to interact with each other as well. Such opportunity adds the peer learning dimension to the presentation which results in your effectiveness as a speaker. However, a great vigilance is required when we subject the audience to any such activity where they will have to interact with each other, lest they lose focus and you lose control on them. It would be better to give them a time limit in which they will have to finish the activity.

An interactive session gives people an opportunity to speak. When they speak, they are thinking and thinking means they are mentally at it – which means they are engaged. Start your presentation by setting expectations from audience. Tell them you want them to interact and ask questions whenever they have any or if you have designated any time for it. Else if you are speaking at some larger venue like a conference where it is not possible to entertain every question, you can take it to the next level wherein you invite people to tweet, blog or post on your Facebook page. This would enhance your credibility by showing that you are available for them and that you would love to hear from them any time after the session.

One evergreen rule to ensure participation is to ask your audience what they think about a particular point. If you are speaking to a smaller group, you can go as far as asking a single person's opinion, not to be followed with mass audience though.

Bring it Home: The subject and all the discussion about it has to be something that audience can relate to. It has to be immediate and local. By saying that I mean whenever we give an example or quote some statistics supporting our statement, it should be about a thing, place, person or situation that audience is aware of. People are not interested in you travelling overseas every time you quote an example because it may be lot different than their state of affairs. Quoting local example and discussing immediate statistics has a personal touch in the sense that audience feel it has to do with them. If I am speaking about the social reforms, people would better relate to me if I discuss Indian Taboos that existed before or exist now rather than social reforms of Europe. In management terminology, we call it "Glocal Strategy". Glocal is a combined word for globalization and localization. That means you could be global in thinking, but you have to act local – *Being Global, Acting Local.*

People are more interested when someone speaks to them about their problems. They primarily need solutions to their own troubles rather than of someone's they know nothing about. So to ensure enhanced engagement we have to speak about whom we are speaking to.

Make it Personal: Doesn't matter if you are an established speaker or someone who has just started, people are always interested in knowing your triumphs and falls. It's perfectly ok to share your experiences about the subject and try to know of audience's as well. The best practice to personalize would be to choose respondents to your questions from every side or dimension of the hall. Picking respondents randomly from every side keeps your audience on toes. It becomes kind of compulsion for them to pay attention to you because they could be asked to share a thought or answer a question any time. This way you can take your audience along and never lose them. Moreover when you ask someone to present their stand on the topic they feel valued and consider themselves being part of the discussion.

Having participated in number of seminars, guest lectures and workshops as an academician, I have noticed a strange behavior in speakers. They give most of their attention to the part of audience that they feel is responding more. This part of audience could be shaking heads to give their nod, be a bit more interactive in first few minutes of the session or sitting very close to the speaker. The speaker behaves as if there is no one else in this room besides this group. This is an act of pure disengagement and speaker is bound to lose major part of his audience. Every human by his very nature demands and deserves attention. He wants to be valued and be spoken to. So a speaker while keeping this focus group on board has to turn his attention to others and keep them all engaged.

Praise and Acknowledge the Contribution: Recognition is tested and successful tool of motivation. If we acknowledge and praise the contribution of people towards any aspect of life, they feel like doing more. We can use this technique to engage our audience very well. Using the words like 'That's great', 'Superb', 'Perfect' to acknowledge any answers or thoughts from your audience goes a long way. This technique works perfectly well for a teacher dealing with students who have to be involved for effective learning. Praise and acknowledgement sets people on fire and they get this feeling of 'I want to do it again ...' It gets them waiting for next opportunity and encourages them to be with the speaker physically and mentally.

At times people would give wrong answer or respond negatively. The speaker has to be careful handling these responses and should not discourage them by words like, 'Sorry Marry, but you are wrong' or something like 'That's totally incorrect, or say, 'Not even close'. These people need to be given a message that they are wrong but in a way that doesn't discourage them from participating further. A speaker can respond like 'Ahaan, let's see if someone else has a different view', or turn to other side of the audience and say, 'Let's see if there is anyone else who thinks that way'. The speaker may as well read the situation and respond accordingly. A perfect mix of kind words delivered in a kind way would help handling this situation.

Break the Inertia: An effective speaker doesn't let his audience go to rest. He would always keep them moving and rolling by using the techniques and skills a communicator should know. Part of this entails to his own activities on the stage and part to what he makes his audience do. For instance, a speaker would never keep the similar tone and pitch for longer durations. Monotony gets boring. He would support his statements by his gestures and body language so that the audience knows a thought has begun or completed. This helps them draw meaning out of it. An established speaker would always change positions on the stage never letting eyes go to rest. An eye going to rest means it's going to sleep.

Being in speaking business for years now, I can realize when my audience is getting bored and when do they need an antidote to wake them up. Or for that matter any frequent speaker can figure out state of his audience from their facial expressions or body movements. And when you see any such thing in people sitting before you, that's the time you need to break the inertia. Give them a brain teaser before moving on to your next point. It sets their brain in motion and inertia breaks. Have a little fun by making a joke. You can also request them to stand up and give them some meditation tips that set their blood rolling. It's not bad for a teacher to have the seats of students changed. After all changing neighbors sets any one in motion!

You can also get them moving by making them stand or sit to show agreement to any of points you make. And if you have enough time and small audience like a class of 20-30 students, you can divide them into groups who share commonality.

Help Them Understand by a Story: Story telling is an art and is undoubtedly one of the best tools to engage the audience. An effective speaker shares stories to achieve multiple goals. A story could be used as a cliff hanger that creates suspense among listeners driving them towards the curiosity of what is happening next. It induces dopamine levels helping people to focus. When a speaker delivers his message by storytelling, he develops the trust and bonding with the audience that enhances the credibility of his message. This trust and bonding is the result of a hormone called Oxytocin which is released when we hear a message with emotional touch. Oxytocin makes us empathetic when we visualize and kind of relate to the story being narrated to us. Storytelling has a great science behind it and is a proven method to make people understand your message.

Every experience that we have to share could become a great story. However, we have to ask ourselves a question before we go on narrating it, and that question is, 'How do I want my audience feel after this story'? It is detrimental because we have to adjust our gestures, tone and body language as per the goal of the story. If for instance my purpose of sharing a story is to motivate the people and have them focus on my message, I would possibly have to look enthusiastic and break my words to create some suspense. I would possibly not say everything in one breath. And now if I have to induce emotions among my audience, I would certainly have to speak in submission and lower my tone.

When a speaker masters the art of storytelling, even a question can be asked in the form of a story. Stories keep people engaged because they like to know the success stories and failures of other ones. They prefer learning through experiences, whether their own or someone else's.

Engaging Through Social Learning: Let's think back on all the seminars, guest lectures and conferences we have attended. How much of everything we heard there do we remember?

Be honest answering this question, nobody is going to check. And now ask this question to as many people as you can and you would see nearly all them reply, in effect, "not much". This is the depressing news for all

37

speakers and something for them to ponder on. When people are asked about the most memorable presentations, they tend to mention the ones in which they were given an opportunity to participate. They remember sessions where there was a lot of interaction with the presenter and among the fellow audience. Why go to people? Ask yourself and see what makes you remember a session. Most certainly, it would be the one filled with enthusiasm and socialization.

We have to design our sessions to facilitate social learning – the learning that occurs through engagement, connection and conversation not just with the speaker, but with peers as well. Participation is actually a lot more fun and active participants learn well and retain it better. The audience that comes out to attend a seminar or conference is generally socializing and outgoing. They prefer the peer learning dimension of the session rather than sitting next to a stranger who remains a stranger till the end. Social learning creates better outcome as participants influence the structure of the session towards something they want to learn. So take the momentum forward and get involved with people and let them get involved with one another.

Non engagement is deadly. Well, that may seem to be a bit of exaggeration, but it holds meaning for a speaker. Your session doesn't have to be a content broadcasting; it has to be a two-way communication. Avoiding interaction with your audience has a potential to hurt you. People don't find it reasonable sitting somewhere for longer when they have nothing to do but listen to someone speaking. They don't want to feel ignored. So give the opportunity to come in and be the part of action.

PRINCIPLE OF GESTURES AND BODY LANGUAGE

Humans as species have evolved to communicate – both verbally and non-verbally. We influence each other not only by 'what we say', but also by 'how we say it'. The message and the content are about what we say, which has to be supported by our innate knack of knowing how to say it, i.e. gestures and body language. As per a research quoted by Toastmasters International, 'more than half of all communication takes place nonverbally'. So people base their judgment of your delivery on what they hear and what they see. Our body language could be the super power that governs the effective delivery of our message. However, it could equally be a distraction fatal for our presentation, doesn't matter how convincing our content is. As public speakers we must project sincerity, earnestness and enthusiasm through our body language by making our actions affirm what we say. In this chapter we would discuss various gestures and know which ones are to be used and where. We will also try to understand how humans use their body parts to communicate and supplement the effectiveness of their message.

Before moving on to discuss the anatomy of various gestures, let's see how positive or negative gestures affect the speaker and the influence they have on audience.

Gestures and The Speaker: Confidence is actually a brain game. You will feel confident if your brain finds you doing something confidently. That means if you can convince yourself that you are using a gesture right, this gesture will add to your confidence. Now, whether audience finds this gesture right or not is altogether a different question. For now we only discuss the effect of gestures on speaker's confidence. Quoting Amy Cuddy, a social psychologist in her Ted Talk "your body language may shape who you are", mere standing in a posture of confidence even when you don't feel confident, can actually boost the feelings of confidence. These gestures which she calls the *power poses* release a hormone called testosterone – a chemical released inside your body that makes you feel confident. Consequently, if you don't use a power pose a different hormone called cortisol is released that makes you feel

39

powerless. Apparently, you won't like to feel less confident at the stage, would you?

We would discuss these positive gestures (power poses) along with their counter poses (negative gestures) in subsequent parts of this chapter. The rationale here is that a speaker doesn't have to leave the gestures and body language to the chance. He needs to think about his postures with conscious mind, practice them adequately till he finds confidence in using them. I may rather put it this way; the relationship between confidence and gestures is not unilateral, it's bilateral. It's not just the established and confident speaker who uses positive or power poses; it's also the use of power poses that makes you a confident speaker.

Gestures and The Audience: It's not only the speaker who is influenced by his gestures and posture positions at the stage. His acts have the big time influence on his audience as well. Openness of the speaker's body language and his proximity to the audience both increase the positive reception. A speaker has to know that his audience first notices the non-verbal part of the communication right from the time when you make your first appearance on the stage. It's the time when you have not even started speaking, but you are already communicating. The effect of your first appearance and initial gestures has a lasting effect on people. And in the very first few moments your audience will adjust to the kind of personality they think you are. For instance, using strong gestures like walking in with enthusiasm reflecting full energy like that of a boy in his early 20s induces adrenaline levels in your audience and they feel equally energetic. Doing so, a speaker is at advantage. People perceive his session to be interactive, full of engagement and actually prepare their mind for engagement.

On the other hand, stepping in as a modest speaker with not enough energy reflecting from your body leaves people guessing. It creates kind of curiosity among people about the message you are going to deliver and how you would begin. The audience becomes a little worrisome about how this session is going to pass. Nonetheless, inducing enthusiasm among your audience or leaving them curious may both work to your benefit, and would depend upon how you start off your verbal part. The purpose here is to know that whatever the gesture we use, it does affect you as a speaker and so it does to the audience.

As mentioned before, we should never let loose of gestures and should always be mindful of what we are doing with our body parts on the stage. Using them right adds to the effectiveness of our delivery, making us a super hero with audience thanking us in the end. However, not using gestures right or being unmindful of them may as well turn us into a laughing stock for people. And unless you are a full time joker you won't like that happen.

Alright, now is the time to learn how to use our body effectively during presentations. We would discuss the anatomy of various gestures that are commonly used by speakers globally and would learn what they mean to us and to our audience. This discussion shall give you a fair idea of body language we need adopt on stage.

Smile: People are generally indifferent to strangers. Unless they see something common in a stranger or are able to relate themselves to the stranger, they won't care what a stranger has to do or to say. When we hit the stage, we are most often strangers knowing nothing about people sitting before us and in turn having them never seen us before. Our goal as a speaker won't be achieved if we remain like strangers throughout. So our first objective would be to break all the differences and move close to audience's heart and mind by presenting ourselves as being one of them. And there is no better way to this than a smile.

Yes exactly, smile that you know of – pulling your lip muscles laterally and arching your eyebrows upwards, that smile!

It's a powerful thing, an outward act of warmth that people can't stop but mirror. Forget about people for a while; see what it does to you. Ask biologists or chemists and they have proven that smiling elicits a chemical reaction in your body – releasing hormones like dopamine and serotonin that literally change the way you feel. We should never lose our smile even if our presentation is meant to induce negative and cold emotions like disappointment, sadness, anger – which is required at times depending on your subject. Because (as put nicely by Mo Waja – Host of Toronto city archive podcast),

"Your smile controls the temperature of the room, and as you lose your smile your room loses its warmth by degrees".

Smile is a universal anecdote making any one feel good. There is a reason why employees interacting with customers at any level are taught to smile, be it a salesman, receptionist, administrative assistant or a call center agent. It creates an instant connection between people. Lack the smile, and you are in the first place distancing yourself from your audience by colder and negative tone.

And now for your audience, smiling is the best way to engage them. They see the harmony and personalization in your smile. And when you

41

see people respond to your smile by a smile on their face, you are at the apex of confidence.

Posture: When it comes to non-verbal communication, people worry far too much about their gestures and body movements on the stage. The concern of self-conscious people being on the stage before a crowd with all eyes focused on them gets intensified. They want to know how to stand there. However, such concern would usually lead to gestures that are unnatural and speaker would never be confident with them. So the first thing we need to do is to be ourselves and look natural on the stage. In this regard, everything that I suggest in this section needs to be owned by speaker and practiced enough till it looks pure and natural.

So to begin with, you won't start roaming around in the very first moment of hitting the stage. Slow down, take a pause and have a look around for couple of seconds. The audience too needs to have a glimpse of a speaker. Even if you start off directly with introduction, I recommend be a little static with a positive posture. And two crucial and very important things about the posture would be to know *How to stand* and *Where to stand*.

How to Stand: Whatever posture you take on the stage, it should reflect confidence and make you feel up. I recommend adopting the posture of dominance and independence especially in the beginning. And that would be standing erect with your backbone straight facing the audience upfront. Try to expose as much of your body as possible. Never turn your back to your audience. Even if you have to refer to the slides and need to look at the projector screen, turn just a part of your body as much as it gets easy for you to look at the screen. Do not stand like a Wonder Woman with hands on the hips, it reflects sheer arrogance. A speaker should as much as possible avoid keeping his hands in pockets anytime during the session, it's informal and little disrespectful to the audience. Imagine your subordinate talking to you with hands in pocket. Further while introducing or in the very first few moments before audience, you should not wrap your arms round your body and also not hang your arms in front with fingers crossed. Hanging arms with fingers crossed is too much of humility and may hamper your confidence level.

Now one may think that's almost everything and feel like I have to do nothing with my arms! Well that's not the case. A speaker can use his hands while starting off. For example, he may use his hand to point at himself while speaking something about himself or at audience while referring to them. He may also use his hands to support his statements like, if he says, "I came from a far off place," he can extend his hand up towards that direction. While a speaker uses his hands to refer to or to point at something, utmost care should be taken not to point finger at audience. Pointing finger at someone is total disrespect and instead we should use our hand with palms upside. For instance, if you want someone to stand up, extend your hand towards him – keep your palm on the upside and create a little inward bend in your palm. Make sure not to keep your palm flat.

Where to Stand: Having participated in number of guest lectures, seminars and student presentations, I have noticed speakers' kind of hiding behind podiums, projector stands and whatever they find close by. A speaker has to make himself completely visible, not just his chest and head. Remember, a bigger font and bigger picture is always attracting. Moreover, you might have noticed speakers or for that matter teachers, leaning against podiums. Well, that's not formal and something we have to avoid. Start from the middle where everyone can see you and then roam around. While roaming around, it's not bad to get close to the audience and teachers can even go down the aisle. As long as you don't go and sit in somebody's lap, getting close to audience works.

While we are discussing where to stand, it's important to know that we should avoid standing in front of distractions, or even getting close to them. Distraction would be something that takes attention off the speaker. Depending on the type of hall or auditorium you are presenting in and its dimensions, you could face many distractions. We would first speak about a common distraction that's ignored by most of the speakers and that is the **projector screen**.

Sitting in front of the screen or even close to it drags the audience attention to it and they would most probably start reading what's on there, not listen to what's being said. The funny part is that some speakers would come just in between the projector and the screen and enjoy the beam on their face. Such speakers become invisible to the audience for a while. If not that, the audience is certainly going to be invisible to them for the time they are in the beam. This has happened to me and I realize how it destroys the rhythm of your speech. However, you could face many settings where projector and the screen have been placed such that a speaker can't avoid coming in between. In such scenarios try lowering your gaze when you are passing in between and find the spots on the stage where you can minimize the exposure and audience can see you. The sole purpose is not to lose the connection with your audience at any moment.

The next distraction that's very common to Indian type classroom settings where electricity can't be trusted much is something that I call the **Sight-full Window**. As seen often, the light goes off and all the temperature controlling stuff stops working and we turn to open window policy for ventilation. Speaking literally, a lot can be happening outside that is totally visible through the widow and can be a big time distraction for the audience. The speaker can avoid this distraction by not moving close to the open window. Not just that, some halls and classrooms have big window panes near the stage and may catch an eye even when closed. The speaker has to make sure these window panes are covered with curtains if there is an efficient artificial lighting system in place. If not so, a teacher or presenter has to avoid getting near them as much as possible.

Now there is this all-time distraction that a speaker and audience carry with themselves. Yes, I am speaking about the **Lifeline device – the mobile device.** I don't think any speaker at any stage would accept being in the middle of interaction and feel his phone vibrating in the pocket, or even bigger mess, hear his phone ringing. It's highly recommended not to display your phone at all anytime during your session, unless you have something to demonstrate of it. A teacher should make a habit of turning it silent before getting in the class. Further, it's not at all wrong to spare a moment and request your audience to turn their devices off for a while. Do this after introducing them to your subject. Make them feel the importance of this session and let them know how this is going to change their thinking, behavior or help them in life. A teacher can let his students know that he doesn't want any distractions and given to the importance of this session, they don't want any distraction either. So it's important to turn the devices off, unless of course, someone is expecting a very urgent call or so.

Furthermore, there could be some other distractions like motivational posters, hanging quotes or even a wall clock that can take audience attention and result in disengagement. All of these distractions are to be figured out in the first few moments of your session. Or as suggested in the first chapter of this book, try to get a glimpse of hall settings in advance.

I can summarize our discussion in following words;

Stand where you catch all eyes,
Stand in a way that everyone feels your confidence.

Audience Posture Matters Too: While a speaker is too much into his body language and gestures, he should not ignore the body language of his audience. There is a lot of immediate feedback in the gestures of your audience. A successful speaker knows his audience and understands every move they make. He knows that for a memorable session audience has to posture positively as well. I believe a speaker should understand the meaning behind the gestures of his audience to know when to adjust his speech and break the flow and when to keep the momentum going – the sole aim being the audience engagement.

Start noticing the audience movements after 15-20 minutes, because they would take this much time to figure out about you as a speaker and the subject. After this time if you see your audience taking notes, that would be a positive sign for you, a sign of engagement. You can figure out their engagement from the responses they give to your statements. For example, shaking the head when you ask an assertive question like **Is that Okay?** Or a question that induces negative response like this one - **'Am I going too fast** (when you know you are not)? One of the best ways to see if your audience is still with you is to notice the response to your emotional statements. For instance, you said something emotional and they are still looking down, you added a humorous anecdote and many of them are not smiling. These are the signs of you losing them and that's where you have to break the inertia and act a little different. Further when you see many of them yawning, it means either the session is boring or has been going on for longer duration. Give them a surprise here, pick some of them randomly and ask for their take on a point you discussed. When you see them giving nod to your statement, that means they agree and have understood it well. You have to look for this nod from every corner of the hall. A continuous eye contact is another sign of engagement. Make sure you look to every side and they in turn have eyes on you.

A speaker should never let his audience adopt a negative gesture. This could be achieved by breaking the flow and introducing a different element in your speech every 15-20 minutes. The different element could be asking a provocative question, sharing a joke, engaging them in an activity or picking some of them for a demonstration. Having people post on your Facebook page or writing to your blog is too far a feedback and doesn't help you control the current session. The best way is to keep noticing your audience gestures and adjust the speech accordingly.

Gestures to Mind: Practically speaking, there is no hard and fast rule for gestures except a few that have a common global meaning. The rest is contingent and needs to be adjusted as per the kind of audience one may have. I mean move to any corner of the world and raise your thumb to anyone, they would know you are wishing them luck or you appreciate what they are doing. Smile is a gesture of personalization and anyone on earth would know this. You point finger at anyone and they would never like it because everyone takes it as disrespect, something done by politicians, not a professional speaker. Keep your hands on hips and pose like a wonder woman, you don't have to tell anyone about your over confidence because you already showed it. Don't focus your eyes on anyone, just let them wander over faces and everyone knows how nervous you are. Or keep turning your back to the audience for one reason or another, they would know you don't want to face them and somehow want to finish your part as quick as possible. Go down the aisle and surprise the people by moving close to them, they would know how you love what you are doing. Handle a question from your audience by completely turning to the person asking the question, they would see your courtesy and realize how confident you are about your answer. These are all the gestures of global commonality and bear the similar meaning everywhere. However, there are some gestures that would mean different to different people. In this section we would discuss some common but very important gestures along with some situational ones.

Eye Contact: There are some gestures and body language poses that are readily noticed by people in the very get go. This is something that no speaker can hide and is adjudged even by a potentially amateur audience. I would rather call such gestures the **'primary gestures'** and would place eye contact in this category. Eye contact helps connecting to people and gives you access to their mind. It snatches audience attention and they find no option but to listen to you and understand you. I would prefer discussing the gesture of eye contact under a separate principle called the **'Principle of focused Eyes'**.

This principle says there is a lot more to eye contact than just the engagement. It's about giving value to people and make them feel honored. It says when you speak, don't just look at a face to get a glimpse of it and then flip on to another face. Instead stop for a while and focus your eyes on that person for 3-5 seconds. There is a philosophy behind this principle. When you focus your eyes on someone, it's like you are talking to them and there is no one else in the hall but the concerned person. It takes people to the height of engagement and they feel how well you are considering their presence. It would sort of personalize the session and makes people feel valued. However, care has to be taken not to exceed 3-5 seconds while looking at someone, because you don't want to look biased or make them feel uncomfortable either. Move on to the next person and follow the principle again. It won't be possible to look at every face in a large crowd; however it certainly does wonders in a class of 30-40 students where you have time and visibility. As discussed in the previous chapter some speakers would turn most of their attention to a group of audience sitting close or whom he thinks are responding fairly. Such speakers are bound to fail on the grounds of this principle because this principle wants you to possibly focus on every face sitting before you, not just a group. You can turn to a single face many times during your session and that would depend on the size of your audience and their proximity to the speaker. You will have to read the hall settings and behave accordingly.

The positive eye contact is the sign of confidence and gives the audience the reason to believe that you are not there just to broadcast the content, but to engage them in something they can benefit from.

Using Hands: The natural position of hands while speaking in public is having them hang neutrally on sides. From there we can bring them to play only when it is absolutely needed. Don't raise your hand unnecessarily for the sake of playing with it. The gesture has to look true to the audience. The secret is to focus completely on getting your message across; your hand would naturally support what you say. You can stand up right now and try hanging your arms on sides and see how it feels. I bet you would feel it being a little awkward initially, but it's perfectly natural. Do remember what I said earlier – you have to practice it and own it. While you start bringing your hands to play, don't use them repetitively for a single gesture. The general rule is that any movement that reinforces your message is good and natural and anything that distracts from it is not. All you have to be a little careful about is to avoid the gestures that you know people won't like. And that could be putting your hands together in a way that creates sound. Don't get me wrong, clapping does work if you have to demonstrate something of it, I mean don't do it repetitively and unconsciously. Further as discussed before; avoid pointing finger at audience especially when you refer to a particular person.

The female speakers need to tie their hair properly, else we find them do nothing with their hands but adjust the hair. It's a major distraction that doesn't just hamper you to get your message across by shaking your confidence; it also gets annoying for people watching. A common problem found mostly with Indian female speakers is putting on the ethnic 'Saree', which is considered completely formal. The trouble is that it never allows you to gesture effectively. I have seen it drifting off the shoulders as and when you try to use your hands to demonstrate something. There have been some speakers though, who would tie it in a way that it doesn't become a hurdle for them. You have to be simple but mindful of everything you present on the stage. The most important visual you can show an audience is your own self and everything about it matters.

The stance of looking natural should not be confused with blissful ignorance of your body movements that some people believe in. We should not completely forget about our hand movements and let our unconscious mind drive them. I mean it is this blissful ignorance that you scratch your lower abdomen in front of your professional audience when you feel a little itchy. It seems natural to do so. However, I don't think you would feel proud of yourself when you watch a recording of this session back home!

We can use our hands to add visual impact to our message. For instance, when we say a number we show it by our fingers. When we underscore the importance of an issue we can use hands to force it. For example, when we say "there is this small thing we need to understand", we can use our thumb and point finger to show how small it is. For bigger things we can stretch our hands wide apart. Further, when you make an emotional statement, put your hand on your heart. It goes with the statements like "I am so grateful for this opportunity to interact with you guys". You can also use your hands to help other keep track of your explanation. Say you are comparing two options A and B. Whenever you speak about option A, raise your right hand. And when you have to mention option B, use your left hand. It would help your audience follow you conveniently.

The purpose here is to use your hand gestures as reinforcement to what you say. And when these two i.e. gestures and words move in tandem, it creates a lasting impact on people and it gets hard for them to disengage.

Go ahead and use your hand naturally, but be mindful of any negative gestures.

Body Movements: Watching a stationary speaker is tedious and we don't have to glue ourselves to one particular spot while speaking. Body movement is most visible kind of physical action that's evident to everyone and this has to be mastered. It calls for attention since a moving object doesn't let eyes go to rest and they follow you inevitably. The general rule to be followed here is that all moves should be purposeful and calculated. Moving for a purpose in tandem with your message enhances your delivery and raises alertness among audience. There are many reasons why one should be in control of body movements, and why do we give it a separate space in our discussion.

First of all, your body movements set your blood rolling and relieve you of the physical tension. Incorporating purposeful movements in your speech can actually help overcome nervousness. Speaking of the second dimension, body movements can reinforce what you say in words. For instance, if you have finished a thought and are going to start another one, move sideways – it implies transition and audience gears up for another thought. Taking a step forward means something important is coming. And similarly taking a step back means conclusion.

However, there is something important I want my readers to know. And it is that you don't have to bind yourself by the general rule of purposeful and calculated movements. I mean there would be situations when you realize you should move, but you don't want your movement convey a message. You take this movement just to avoid eyes going to rest. For example, a thought or opinion goes too long and you realize getting static. In this situation you can move to a different place even when you don't mean anything of transition, conclusion or importance. Our purpose is not just to create a harmony between movement and the message, it is effective delivery. Anything that contributes to it naturally is accepted.

Finally, your body movements help you in audience engagement. You can take a step close to them and notice their response. People prefer proximity when it comes to face to face interactions and I believe speaking publicly in a seminar, conference or as a teacher in class is nothing more than a face to face interaction.

Anyways, take care about getting carried away by your movements. The beginners do get carried away. Enthusiasm drives them so much that they go on rocking, racing and swaying without realizing what they are doing. So ideally, try to seek some middle ground where you move your body enough to keep listener's attention, yet not enough to distract them.

Facial Expressions: When it comes to nonverbal speaking, face communicates more clearly than any other body organ. People can easily recognize the feelings like fear, confusion, happiness, anger, sadness and interest simply by observing your face. They will use your face as barometer to find out your inner state, so your face should reflect exactly the feeling your message carries. It's not actually your narration that tells people how to feel, it's facial expressions they read that helps them decide what speakers wants them to do. For example, what if you say, "I lost an opportunity to work at an esteemed academic position in higher education, because I couldn't deliver well in demo class", and you wanted people feel a little emotional? What kind of facial expression should you wear – a smile or a contemptuous sneer that clearly shows you still feel bad about that day? Go on and smile, you will find people laughing at this fall of your life. And now try and show some disappointment on your face, people will get altogether a different message. They would realize the importance of effective communication in their lives, something you probably wanted them to do.

"The meaning doesn't lie in words.
It lies in the feelings that you generate while you deliver those words".

You could have multiple gestures communicating similar message. However, adopt the one that goes with your face. The best way to know which one suits you is to speak in front of a mirror and evaluate your expressions. Some communication experts even suggest delivering full speech in front of mirror using expressions only, without saying a single word. Remove the expression that you think doesn't belong to your face. People don't want to listen to someone who makes faces; they would better go with someone who is real. Avoid unnecessary expressions like licking or biting your lips, tightening the jaws and dragging your lips laterally. It would only burn the calories of your facial muscles and soon you would feel the fatigue. Know that smiling no doubt is the most positive facial expression, but too much of it becomes inconsequential and audience may lose the seriousness of your message.
The key is to allow the harmony develop between your words and facial expressions and look as natural as possible. Faking words gets easy at times, faking expressions doesn't.

Looks and Appearances: The most benevolent thing you can present to your audience is your own self. And the way you present yourself to them goes a long way. Believe it or not, people do notice every bit about a speaker, be it a veteran in his late 70s or a young handsome dude in his early 20s. Your appearance conveys a powerful visual message and strongly influences how people judge you. The fact is that you can't change your physical attributes like height, age or kind of face you have.

But you can certainly enhance your looks through grooming, physical conditioning and proper attire.

While getting dressed for your program, you should know the kind of audience you are going to face. The dressing preferences vary with location, society and culture of the place. Try to be a well-dressed person, if not the best dressed person in the hall. If you are going to a formal gathering where people wear suits and dresses, make sure you wear the same. Don't get carried away by the compliments you expect from people, wear something that first makes you a confident speaker. People will compliment anything for the sake of formality. Better dress up in front of a sincere friend of yours, your wife or a partner before taking a final call. The clothing has to be clean, nicely tailored and made to measure.

For women, don't wear suits or jewelry that glitters or creates sound while you move or gesture. Else it would be a big time distraction for audience. For Indian women who prefer wearing 'Payals' (an ornament tied to ankle – creates what I may call a feministic sound while walking) in normal routine, avoid wearing it during your speeches and programs where you are the center of attraction. And of course, your high heels! I would rather suggest no heels on stage.

I can't stop but praise Toastmasters when they say, "for the same reason of avoiding distraction, empty your pockets of bulky objects or things such as pocket change or keys that produce audible sounds when you move". I have noticed this keenly; even humpy wallets become a distraction. They further suggest watching your diet and exercising regularly because audiences like speakers with good health and physical vitality.

Beyond the gestures we have discussed so far, there are few that would mean different to different people. The speaker has to be vigilant about the kind of audience and their belief system. A strong gestures of widening arms may seem enthusiastic to young audience, however a little offensive to elderly. The meaning we attach to gestures is the product of our cultural upbringing. People in India generally nod their heads up and down to show agreement and laterally to say no. However in some parts they would nod sideways and actually mean yes. Similarly, join your forefinger and thumb to make a circle would mean perfect in western nations, but obscenity in reserved parts of the world. A good rule of thumb is to focus on the message and let gestures follow. You have to be genuinely yourself and not try to create a gesture that nobody understands. Or you don't have to copy other speaker's gestures, else it looks totally artificial. Just as words don't have the meaning of their own, the context gives them meaning. Similarly the meaning people get out of gestures would depend on the message and the context.

So stand strong, gesture effectively and mind your audience.

PRINCIPLE OF PITCH AND PACE

Having learned a bit about the nonverbal part of communication from the discussion in the previous chapter, we shall now see how to make the verbal part more effective. This is something every speaker of any level is more concerned about - I mean every beginner and an established speaker. Even though **'what people hear'** contributes only 50% to their judgment about you – the rest 50% being **'what they see'** from you, the verbal part remains the main driving force when it comes to preparing for the session.

Written language has its own rules and array of symbols like commas, full stops, exclamation and questions marks, letting people know when a thought has begun or ended, when the discussion on a topic finished and when was the new one taken up. However, in speaking people are completely dependent on speaker. We use entirely different symbols to show the intensity of our thought to the audience and let them know what part of our speech demands more attention. We use effective speaking techniques to add power and vitality to our words. We use the flow, pitch and pace of our words to tell people what do we mean and how do we mean it.

I have a firm belief that the moment you learn how to play effectively with the flow, pitch and pace of your words, you would already be an effective communicator. And I dedicate this chapter of my book to this learning of yours. Here in we would discuss the paralanguage and learn how to manipulate our speaking style to grab the control on audience, make them listen and leave them wanting more.

Mind the Flow: Every speech has a structure that guides the speaker through the session. It's a well drafted framework joining various parts of speech that helps a speaker in not losing the track. It is this structure or framework that gives your speech a flow, which is adjudged by a clear and well connected beginning, the middle and the end. A speaker for example needs to know what he has to say about himself before moving on to introducing his topic. If he has designed his introduction part well, he would say only what seems important and not bang about his

53

achievements and get carried away for minutes. By the time he realizes going too far, he has already played down the flow of his speech. A positive flow entails knowing *what to say*, *when to say* and *how much to say*. A general rule is to grasp the structure of your speech and practice it well before going to the stage. If possible, record your speech couple of times and see if you are deviating from the structure. While listening to your recording, ask yourself this question - should your audience really hear this? If the answer is no, remove this sentence right then and see if replacement is possible.

Regulating the flow of speech is like connecting various dots and making a fabulous structure out of dots that shocks every one. An effective speech is not about delivering thoughts and ideas at random. There has to be a perfect connection between every statement you make and audience should be in a position to comprehend the meaning behind it. I suggest doing the following to regulate the flow of your words.

Know Your Subject: It's undoubtedly very important to know what you are talking about. You won't find any rhythm discussing a topic that you have no clue of. Effective public speaking and blasting session demands homework - be it days of research or tens of hours of study and a practice. While training a group of my students for communication, I once told them that you should hit the stage with full confidence. And this boy stood up and asked, Sir, "How can I get this confidence when I have never been to stage before"? That seemed to be a legitimate question which I later came to know in subsequent sessions, bothers many others. My answer was something that had worked for me and I believe is going to work for you. I further believe, it must have worked for him as well. I replied, "A speaker gets first spark of confidence from his preparations". There is this golden rule of old; that if you do not understand something by yourself, there is no way you can make others understand it.

When you know it, you can say it. And when you say it well, others understand it well.

Review and Preview: This technique works really well for longer sessions especially a teaching session. Before we move on to the next topic, we should summarize what we discussed so far and briefly introduce the audience to the new topic. I remember one of my mentors telling me about making the class effective. He said, "If your class is of 60 minutes, spend first 10 minutes reviewing what you discussed yesterday, 40 minutes on your topic today and rest 10 minutes to preview what's coming tomorrow". I cherish this advice and would praise him for life because this technique worked for me big time, not just in a teaching class but in other speaking platforms as well.

Stick to Your Topic: There is something very common between philosophers, and it is that they are pretty hard to understand. These fat knowledge guys have so much to speak about that they often leave the listeners in lurch. Their speech structure is more like having one thousand dots to be joined in just one square foot space. The funny part being that they somehow join these dots, but lines so ride on one another that no one knows how they did it. I mean you ask anyone coming out of philosophical session, 'what was it all about'? The guaranteed answer is going to be − 'it was about almost everything'. But then ask them, 'what did you learn'? The answer for the most part would be − "nothing concrete".

Having vast knowledge of multiple domains is not a bad thing; it's a virtue one could have. However, inability to boil it down to its elementary essence and giving it a shape can be quite sloppy. So a speaker has to be clear in thinking and should not toggle between topics. A thoughtless transition among various subjects makes it tough for audience to follow along.

A speaker may have enormous knowledge of the subject. However, the essence of being an effective speaker lies in being choosy about your knowledge sharing. So stick to your topic and do not beat around the bush. People would rather prefer hearing one thing and understand it than being exposed to dozens and comprehend none.

Evaluate your Statements: Every statement differs from another in terms of importance, intensity and weight. There would be sentences that would just be the part of ongoing discussion and won't mean completion of the topic or transition to another one. Such sentences would require you to keep continuity in the flow. For example, you say, "Business students are supposed to have effective communication skills. They need to work on it". When you say 'They need to work on it' and you want them just to hear it, you don't have to manipulate the flow of your words. However, if you want them to feel the importance of working on communication skills, you won't keep the continuity in your flow. You would probably stop before you spell it out and even change the tone of your voice. Stopping before saying it or changing the tone breaks the inertia and indicates something different is coming − something that speaker wants you to listen to or something that needs to be heard. A speaker has to evaluate the value of his words or statements in terms of how he wants the audience to feel or react and adjust his flow accordingly.

Mastering the flow and knowing where and how to break or keep it is a major challenge. A speaker overcomes this challenge by consistent speaking. Once under control, it becomes a major weapon to fight the battle of public speaking. Breaking the flow has its own philosophy. Imagine a sudden silence after 3 minutes of continuous noise the speaker makes. I have noticed this silence waking up those who are otherwise sleeping. The flow is clearly the function of your statements and words. Never would a speaker break the flow if sentences or its parts have some adjoining meaning. I believe the following example would help me clear what I am trying to say.

A speaker wanted to say that we should never miss a chance to hit the stage whenever it comes our way. He asked a question to see who in audience is ready to grab this opportunity. But he did not intend to bring anyone to the stage while he asked the question. Let me tell you how his lack of knowledge about breaking or keeping the flow created a little mess for him. The question he asked was, **"Would you like to come to the stage, if you are given a chance?"** This question was supposed to be asked in one go, but he broke his flow and said, "Would you like to come to the stage?" Before he could have said 'if you are given a chance', this lady he was looking at stood up and thought the speaker wanted her to come to the stage. The speaker later cleared it and said I was only looking for a nod. He further apologized for taking a longer pause that created the misunderstanding.

Practice Your Speech: There are speakers who believe in spontaneity and magic on the stage and do not bother practicing their speech. Unfortunate for them and more so for audience, such speakers don't always hit it right. What usually happens is that such speakers bounce unpredictably from one topic to another and don't find any ground. This is usually the tale of established speakers like senior professors and organizational higher ups. However, this is something a beginner has to abstain from. A speaker has to know that his initial sessions help him a long way to build confidence and pave the way for his future effectiveness.

As much as possible, a speaker should practice and try his speech and make sure he doesn't deviate from the planned structure of it. This might as well be done alone. However, it's recommended to practice your speech in front of a trusted colleague, a family member or a sincere friend. Practicing helps us to know the flow and that which sentence has to be delivered in what manner. If a particular sentence doesn't fit in well, we could adjust it, remove it or attach a different emotion to it. The ultimate purpose being its effective reception by audience and generating desired response.

Play with Words: A little distortion with the words works well for a speaker. By distortion I mean you can play with the syllables of some words and pronounce them a little differently than how they are supposed to. This however shouldn't be done quite often, lest your audience thinks your knowledge of language is not at par. For instance a speaker says, "The advantage of controlling the flow is so big that a speaker can't help but learn how to master it". In this sentence we can distort the pronunciation of 'so' by adding a couple of more Os as suffix to it. That way, our sentence would be like, "The advantage of controlling the flow is **sooo big** – and then the rest. Playing with the words would mean you can stretch it, contract it or break it into syllables and spell it slowly. Similarly, you would notice the word **"Can't"** is spelled as can't by almost all speakers around the globe. However, breaking this word into **"Can Not"** gives altogether a different impression. It reflects seriousness of the statement and helps breaking the monotony and hence is a way to break the flow.

Overcome forgetfulness: Undoubtedly, one of the major reasons of people being weary about facing the public is their forgetfulness. I have met number of students who forward only one reason of their nervousness and that's forgetting. It's not just that people are worried about forgetfulness; they actually forget when they face the crowd. I believe its quiet humane and all of us face this trouble at some level. However, effectiveness lies in what speakers do when they forget. Should we apply full breaks on our speaking vehicle and do nothing but wait for the word to come our mind? Or do something that renders forgetfulness irrelevant? Well, I think you and I are like minded and we would both go with the second option – we should do something about it. So, here is the antidote to overcome the ill effects of forgetfulness. This is something that has always worked for me, if I ever forgot. And I call this, the **"Principle of Alternation"**. If something slips off your mind, don't wait there; find an alternate way of saying it. You don't want the dead air play in while you speak, else it plays down your performance. The alternate way could be altogether a different word or statement but closely related to forgotten word or statement in terms of meaning. If for instance you wanted to say, "A speaker should hit the stage with confidence and enthusiasm" and you forgot the word enthusiasm. Don't stop there; try to look for an alternate word of same meaning like energy or zeal. However, as happens very often with beginners, if you don't get any word as replacement – start over the complete sentence in a different way with totally new look up. Like in our example we can say, "We need to show energy and confidence while coming to the stage". The purpose is to avoid the distortion in the flow and not lose confidence.

Besides the flow of speech, the pitch and pace of speaking form the two important constituents of paralanguage. In the next part of our discussion, we would see how it matters when we say, 'watch your tone'. Put it rather simple, we would learn a great deal about voice modulation and its effect on people listening to us.

Watch Your Tone: Rightly so, because our tone does something to the person at the other end. It makes him feel the particular way. The voice we give to our words is amazingly a vital tool that could bring people close who are otherwise worlds apart. It may as well push them miles away. Just as the tone of your partner's voice can instigate an argument or hurt feelings in you, the wrong tone in public speaking can also put your audience off. The mere tone of our message accounts for more than 38 percent of our message effectiveness in public. And on phone, it goes to 80 percent. Selecting a tone for your delivery would primarily depend on two things - the kind of message and the type of audience.

Think about your message; is this something serious that requires warm and authoritative tone? Or something meant to excite and inspire people, requiring a lighter tone and a higher pitch. Analyze your message and adopt the tone that fits in well to it and looks completely natural. A simple way to go about this is to keep practicing and recording your speech until you find the fitting tone that conveys the desired emotions behind the message. Getting a little finer into our discussion, an effective session would require us to adjust the tone as per words, leave aside the sentences or message as whole. We have to look for the keywords in the sentences and emphasize on them. If we don't do that, the sentences become dull, flat and create less of an impact.
The next thing that has the great influence on the kind of tone a speaker adopts is the type of audience. If the people you are interacting with are from business fraternity, your tone might be that as professional and

authoritative. However, if you are targeting teenagers like that in a class, your tone has to be a bit more light hearted and quirky. You won't be proud of using high pitch in your session with veterans and retirees. And at the same time the crowd in their twenties won't appreciate your soft monotony. Irrespective of the kind of audience, the flat, dull and monotone will only take your message to the deaf ears. There has to be some enthusiasm, energy and variation in the tone of your voice to keep people engaged.

The Science of Tones: The tone of your voice has to do with the musical aspect of your voice. So what makes a piece of music soothing and worth listening to? I believe the variation in its pitch, volume, pace and emphasis. If you can control these four aspects, you will certainly leave people wanting more. When it comes to what some experts call as Tonology – understanding tones, we get to know about two dimensions. One of which is perfectly under your control and the next one is not. For the sake of understanding these two in relation to one another, we would first discuss the dimension that's not under our control.

The Uncontrollable Dimension
I am speaking about the vocal cords, something natural and beyond your control. It does matter and gives an edge to some speakers. For instance, some people have the natural warm and attractive voice quality that influence people positively. And the others have that shrill voice with high pitch that looks irritating. The Department of psychology, University of Pittsburg, USA makes clear in one of their researches that people make instinctive judgment of speakers based upon their natural voice quality. Specifically speaking, people with deeper voices are considered authoritative. Now that may cause a little disappointment to some, thinking they don't have the deeper voice. So, are they losing out? Well, I don't think so. There are speakers, many of whom I have listened to, who don't have this natural blessing, but they are more effective than even those with deeper voices. Looks like a breather, right? Now, you may ask, what do these people do to overcome this so called natural lag? The answer lies in the second dimension. We can effectively mitigate the effects of not-so-blessed tone if we work on the second dimension.

The Controllable Dimension
A celebrity voice coach Renee Grant-Williams in her book, " Voice Power: Using Your Voice to Captivate, Persuade and Command Attention" rightly puts it as, "most of us take our voices for granted. This

is the voice I was born with, so this is the voice I'm stuck with". True, there is no way we can completely restructure our vocal chords, but we can certainly improve various other aspects of our voice. This is perfectly under your control and if managed well, helps even those who lack natural attractiveness in their voice. It is the Paralanguage – something about your vocals, but beyond the verbal language. It is the understanding of the **"VEP Model"** – that means understanding the effects of Volume, Emphasis and Pace in your speech. We will learn about them all one by one and see how we can use them to our benefit.

Volume: It is the general loudness of your voice – loud enough to be audible by one and all. However, I don't think the volume should only be about the audibility. It should create an effect on people and match the environment of the hall. The level of volume you choose for your words needs you to consider some important factors. A speaker should not follow his wills and whims when it comes to adjusting the volume. Take note of the following factors, it shall guide you volumes about volume.

1. Mode of Communication: If you are speaking on a microphone, your voice is obviously going to reach to everyone sitting in the hall even with low volume. You don't want to beat and burst their eardrums by using your circus master volume, do you? When microphone is in place there is greater possibility that speakers have been adjusted wisely at perfect distances covering the entire audience. So a speaker doesn't have to worry about the audibility at all. He should rather concentrate on clarity and effect of his voice on people. Now since we have introduced microphone into our discussion anyways, I would like you to know some etiquettes of handling the microphone.

- If the microphone is fixed, check for the possibility of it being adjusted to your height and proximity. I bet you won't like to create an arc of your back for your hour long speech. Make sure it is adjusted in a way where you can gesture effectively and maintain a confident posture. Trust me; I have seen speakers who would never ask anyone to adjust lectern or microphone for them. Instead they would adjust themselves to these tools and stand as if they are serving some punishment.
- If you have a cordless microphone, you have freedom for the most part. But even there, be careful of handling it. Don't lift it too high as if you are a star performing in a concert. Keep it lower and little vertical with its mouthpiece against your chin.

- Don't hold it where is hides much of your face. Remember, people want to see who is speaking, not just hear.
- Keep it at some distance from your mouth, else people can tell you how many times you breathed in and out. Moreover, it reduces noise and helps in clarity.

Now, if you do not have a microphone as in contemporary Indian classes, you may have to turn your volume a little higher. Turn it only as much higher as it looks natural. Don't sound like shouting and beating people, it is a professional gathering anyways. Furthermore, we run out of calories early on if we use unnaturally high volume.

2. Size of the Audience: This is another factor that would influence your decision of volume selection. A large gathering spread horizontally from left to right or vertically from front to back would require you to be a bit more audible. Further, in such gatherings, especially in the ones spread horizontally, you would have to be careful about the body movements as well. You can not turn away from one side while you look at the other side; else the abandoned side hears little of what you say. A speaker would require maintaining the position where he is equally visible and audible to both left and right sides of the audience. Such type of audience puts a binding on your stage utilization. However, that's where the fun begins. Such situations help you develop innovative and contingent postures by demanding you to work a little more towards audience engagement. And of the small gatherings, you can be yourself. Use the natural tone and low volume to create warmth in the hall. You can be more compassionate and more engaging.

3. Requirement of the Message: The first two aspects had more to do with the audibility of your voice. This one however takes a different route and demands volume to be adjusted to engage your audience and avoid monotony. There are certain words or sometimes complete sentences that require special attention from audience and special focus from speaker. The communicator emphasizes on these words by spelling them out at higher volume. The complete sentence bases it meaning on these words and speaker never wants people to miss them. For example, in a sentence like, "You *have* to take pains of working on your communication, because it's ultimately *you* who is benefitting from it". In this sentence the words *you* and *have* need the emphasis and hence require higher volume while delivering.

The next component of the VEP model after volume is the emphasis. Part of this has already been discussed in the third aspect of the volume adjustment. In this section we would learn a bit more about the messages that need emphasis.

Emphasis: This would require you to understand the content and structure of your message and find out the keywords that demand comparatively more attention. When you emphasize only on keywords, the first help you get from it is getting rid of the monotony. So when you vary your tone, you inject life and energy into your message. Emphasis on keywords doesn't let your message go flat and it keeps audience on their toes and creates restlessness. Close your eyes for a moment and think of a speaker who you think is a great communicator. No don't just read it, do it for yourself and tell me, isn't it true that he doesn't speak in flat tone? Don't you feel energy and dynamism in the way they use their voice and in stress variation over words they speak? Now on the opposite side, we all notice people who take off with a particular tone and land with the similar tone with absolutely no fun in between whatsoever. Hearing such speakers, happiness sounds no different than sadness. They would say bomb and chocolate, peace and war, smile and tears – all in similar tone. Now think about it, what effect does it have on your ability to focus on content when you hear such monotone and lifeless voice?

A speaker needs to know his message content and understand the different weight each sentence carries in overall message. A sentence meant to induce negative emotions like sadness and anger has to sound different than the one inducing positive emotions like smile and happiness. Consequently, we need to emphasize on them accordingly.

Pace: Finally, the part of the controllable dimension that can turn you into a speaker worth listening to is the speed with which you deliver your words. Some experts suggest being a little slow and let people swallow everything you give them. However I believe the speed should be optimal, where you give your audience enough time to digest your words and at the same time not look lethargic in your delivery. For sure, many of you must be thinking about taking the middle ground then, right? Well, that's not what I mean. The solution to the problem of speaking too fast or being too slow is not the middle ground. It is varying the speaking rate as per your audience and content needs.
A speaker has to ask this question, "Do I speak too fast that gives people hard time to understand me?" or "Am I too slow that audience can sense

no energy and life in my speech?" An easy way to find answer to this question is to record your own voice. Recording gives you the baseline understanding of how you should sound and what pace you should speak with. Don't share these recordings with anyone if you are not comfortable, especially if you are a beginner. It is for your self judgment and gives you the opportunity to analyze your own voice effects like what pace goes well with what sentence. A speaker can try different tones and paces for his words and see which one creates the maximum impact on audience.

Still confused of your pace? Come out of electronic recordings. Speak before someone you trust. Tell them to give you an honest and unbiased feedback. I try to know this from my students by allowing them to write a blind and open ended feedback about various voice aspects in general and pace in particular. By calling it a blind feedback, I mean let them be anonymous. That way, students are not worried about grades you give them and they speak out their mind freely.

Why Worry About Pace? Studies have shown that pace of our speech depends on our culture, geographical location, gender, subject matter, emotional state and audience. Consequently, we all would speak at varying paces because we are not similar on these criteria. Take some time and listen to the speakers you think are well established in speaking business. One thing you are certainly going to notice in them is that their speech rate is different. The problem doesn't lie in having different natural pace; it lies in not being able to adjust it to the situations. You could be just fine in getting your point across to the local crowd, but find yourself in odd situation when you leave your home crowd. Quoting Jim Moore while answering the question, 'How does pace of speech affect communication?' We begin to run onto the reefs of misunderstanding, misinformation, and incomplete communications when we apply our home-grown, locally-flavored speech habits and preconceptions to the world outside our comfort zone. This could be easily taken care of by knowing our speech patterns, particularly pace, and adjusting it to the new situation that could be a new location, a different subject matter or a different audience.

People are generally not conscious about their habitual speaking speed, especially if they are understood by those listening. Their speech could only be considered too fast or too slow if they come out of their normal environment. Apparently, you don't always want to stick to a particular audience or similar subject matter. You want to room around, find new avenues, new people and find different taste to the life. And if you share my taste, you don't want to be a regional speaker, you like to go global. If that is the case, we need to worry about our pace and learn to adjust it.

What Influences the Pace? As we say it in Management, the problem recognized is problem half solved. To master the speed with which our words flow, we have to know in which situations we get speeded up and what slows us down. Generally, as happens with us all, we speed up when we are excited, nervous and passionate about something. So, while you speak and encounter situations that could lead to these feelings, that is when you need to take a pause and go as natural - lest you would be called the "motor mouth". A speedy delivery gets effective at times like when you have some great news to share. However, effectiveness lies in the fact that this is not something we should always stick to. This might as well look a bit strange but people pace up their gestures, not just their words when they are excited or nervous. Such speakers move their eyes quickly from one face to another and their hands give in to some kind of sudden restlessness. This restlessness breaks the harmony between gestures and the words. So, even if you do manage to slow down your speaking speed, make sure your gestures follow.

In contrast, people speak slower when they have some significant idea to share that's important and serious. When you speak slowly, you are actually telling people, "Hey, you need to know this. So listen up". You don't have to do this very often though, else you fail to break the ice and audience gets familiar with your speech pattern. They would eventually lose interest if you make them wait on your words over and over again.

The Optimal Pace: One may ask then, what pace should we adopt? Is it the normal pace, like not so fast and not that slow either? No, that's not the solution. Rather, the optimal pace is one that has flexibility. Which means that speaker should be able to match his pace appropriately with speech content and ability of audience to comprehend it. The *one-size-fits-all* approach doesn't fit in the public speaking. The goal should be to adopt the pace that resonates with people, no matter where you are from or to whom you are speaking. People will absorb and retain a lot more information if the speaker accepts and appreciates the difference between people, and tries to adjust his pace accordingly.

When I was learning about pace and its use in public speaking, I came across an interesting analogy. It cleared my confusion about optimal pace to a greater extent. I believe it would help you as well.

Imagine you are taking your audience on a journey. Your speech (content or subject) is the vehicle that carries them along and you are the driver.

Now, you have the choices. You can drive through so fast that scenery blurs and they can't see anything through windows. While you drive forward, they are gazing through the back window trying to figure out what they missed and where they are. One by one they all get dizzy and sit quietly waiting for the ride to stop. Or by contrast, you can drive so slowly that your passengers (audience) want to come out of the vehicle and walk. However, if you are a responsible driver you would continually adjust your speed as per the road conditions (speech content) and the needs of your passengers (audience). There would be places on the road where you will have to slow down or stop altogether either for your needs or for that of your passengers. And there would be places where you push the accelerator a little harder and give them an exciting thrill.

While most people get to know three kinds of drivers from this analogy, I can see four of them. And I want to finish this discussion by asking you this question - which one do you want to be?

- One who whirls them through very fast?
- One who drives very cautiously?
- One who takes the medium or normal speed?
- Or the one who adjusts his speed to the road conditions and passenger needs?

Altering our speech pattern seems challenging. And why should it not be so, the habitual speed of our words is deeply engrained in us. Growing up in a society we soak up everything around us, even the speech rate of our elders. Our native speed feels natural, comfortable and right. However, we can overcome this challenge and all that it needs is awareness, effort and practice.

PRINCIPLE OF HIDDEN EXPECTATIONS

All the discussions we have been through in the previous chapters are obvious and important for the successful execution of our speech. Every speaker no matter the level tries to know about them and more or less believes in mastering them. And it has to be that way, because these principles are detrimental in your speech effectiveness. However, there is something beyond these five principles that almost no communication expert speaks of. Of all the books, research articles, blogs, websites, audios and videos or for that matter live speakers I have consulted, I didn't see any expert speaking much about them. These are some hidden expectations your audience sets from you. We never get to know these expectations because it doesn't reflect from their facial expressions and body language. Moreover, this is something we never ask anyone about, because all of us are supposed to meet these expectations by our very nature of being humans. No body reveals them, but deep down in the heart of hearts we expect them from every speaker. And the moment speaker falls apart on any of these, he loses all his credibility. The irony being that he doesn't even know about his loss.

These are four expectations and "Julian Treasure" in one of his TED videos calls them as **'HAIL' – Honesty, Authenticity, Integrity** and **Love**. We can easily understand the value underlying these four words by just asking ourselves one simple question, "Where do I want to be on the continuum of HAIL"? Imagine you are a member of an audience, what do you mean when you say a speaker should be honest, authentic, loving and the person with integrity? We will try to answer this question in this part of our discussion and learn how we can develop these four humane attributes in our speech.

Honesty: This is what I used to hear when I was in my primary classes – 'Honesty is the Best policy'. It really turned out to be the best policy in every aspect of life, more so in public speaking. People prefer listening to someone who is more real and seems to have limits to his knowledge. In fact they relate more to someone who looks human, not some wizard who knows it all. Honesty in public speaking means being honest in knowledge sharing. You don't have to fake your knowledge. Deliver what's right. Don't exaggerate on your words; a rational audience always looks for short, clear and honest information.

We have to be little more worried about this part when it comes to teaching business. A responsible teacher never lies just to create embroidery over his statements. If you know the answer to the questions your student poses at you, be confident to clear it. And if you are not sure of the answer, be more confident to say I will have to check this. Honesty is to know and accept the limits to your information. It is, 'not answering the question' than 'answering it wrong'. When people give you the most precious moments of their life and they come to listen to you; there is this expectation that every story, statistics, example or any information you share with them is true, and that it's going to help them.

There would be situations when speaker lies or misinforms his audience and no body would get to know this. However, it is the speaker who is at odds. When you know you are sharing wrong information, the first thing it does to you is the erosion of your own confidence. Because you know you don't mean it. Further, in this age of information facts don't hide for longer. People would ultimately know the truth from one source or another. So, how about your credibility? Rest assured, a speaker can make his session blasting and booming by saying something that doesn't find its base anywhere in books or literature. But I believe this is not the last time you want to speak, is it? You want to feel good about being an authentic speaker, someone whose knowledge can be tested and verified. You want to be trusted and never let people in a doubtful situation. Remember, once dishonest is ever dishonest.

Authenticity: There is this popular misconception prevailing that training people in authentic communication teaches people how to perform authentically. As if there are some techniques speakers need to know to look genuine. Well, there aren't any. And if there were some, we would possibly be dealing with the acting world, not the public speaking. People somehow believe that authentic public speaking requires us to adopt the speaking style or personality that's distant from our natural way of speaking. If you start choreographing every single gesture you make, it won't be just prohibitively time consuming; you would also miss the very essence behind your message – which was to induce a particular response or a thought in people. No amount of rehearsal or scripting can actually make you look genuine. Being genuine and authentic requires you to be perfectly you.

67

The advice of "fake it till you make it" from Amy Cuddy's recent TED Talk that I referred to earlier may be used as a temporary and emergency strategy. However, this is not something you can always stick to. The advice is to know your lag, work on it and create a better version of yourself. Quoting 'Millie Baker' and 'Daniel Kingslay' in their article "Authentic Public Speaking", "There is a real risk with this kind of thinking that we develop superficial layers of performance confidence to get by, grow to believe them ourselves, and then wonder why, deep down, we still feel like a fraud". But, don't get me wrong. When I say be genuine and be you, I don't mean to go completely naked on stage. It is not at all inauthentic to choose what we reveal. You may need couple of layers to feel confident and safe. What I really mean is that we need to have that basic disposition towards being authentic and connecting with people. It is showing some aspects of your personality that you would otherwise show up in a private relationship. It is being human, displaying some of the sensitivity, humor, vulnerability, surprise and emotions - something that a human does to connect with other humans. Quoting 'Brene Brown' in her TED talk on vulnerability, "we are hardwired to connect with others; it's what gives purpose and meaning to our lives".

There is a reason why so many established professors, key note speakers in conferences and other people at esteemed speaking positions can't still find an ear regardless of how perfectly rehearsed or skilled they are. It is because they look "calculated", "phoned in", "insincere" and "not real". You would sometimes wonder putting in such a great effort and engaging people to the maximum, why couldn't you see that charm on their faces you wanted? Well, probably you were rehearsed, not authentic. As 'Nick Morgan' Suggests in his article published in Harvard Business Review, "How to Become an Authentic Speaker" – Try to be open, there is not much chance of communication in being defensive. Try to connect to your audience - Don't let listeners slide away into their thoughts instead of following yours. Be passionate about your topic - Focus not on what you want to say but on why you're giving the speech and how you feel about that. Finally, try to listen – discovering audience's emotional state would be most important during the presentation.

Integrity: Here is another abstract that speakers mostly don't think of, but people always demand it, though unconsciously. You could be a wonderful and dynamic speaker possessing amazing presentation skills. But should you lack integrity, anything you say or do would be a mere lie. So, what is this Integrity? You could find many answers to this question ranging from total honesty with your audience to effective knowledge of your subject. However, I believe the very meaning of integrity lies in "Value Giving". It sums up the ideas of many communication experts and leads to a comprehensive meaning. A speaker needs to consider two dimensions of value giving – Value to audience and value to himself.

We need to respect the people in attendance and value their presence. This could be done by acknowledging any contribution from them in the form of participation in activities and answers to any of your questions. Giving value to your audience lies in realizing the time and efforts they are investing to be present there and in turn giving them something to cherish and something that helps them throughout life. Honesty in knowledge sharing leads to integrity in part and this could be achieved by knowing your subject well. The point to take note of here is that people don't expect you to know everything about the topic chosen. However, you should certainly be the one knowing more than anyone else in the hall. This is where speaker finds value for himself – the second dimension of value giving. There is nothing worse than talking to people about a subject of which they know more than you. Integrity lies in doing your research and learning as much as possibly you can about what you are going to speak. Imagine the embarrassment if you could not answer the question that many in audience could.

However, hold on for a while. With all that being said, I don't mean to show off your knowledge or know-how. Integrity demands balance in your confidence and submission. Should you be more submissive, people think you don't know. And if you display enough of the confidence, they find you inaccessible. Don't get carried away by my statement that, 'you should know more than anyone else in the hall' so much so that you start lying and faking your knowledge. If you are not sure of the answer, tell them you will find out and get back to them. If this was a one time session where you could not possibly see this guy again, ask for the phone number or an email. You will be surprised to see how appreciative people are when you treat them with honesty.

Integrity is simple not cheating people or yourself. Relationships are built on being honest with people and that's the fundamental tenet of communication. So be honest, transparent and open – this leaves them praising you rather than questioning or doubting your integrity.

Love: Many public speakers don't spare even a minute to think about what people want to hear, they assume they know it already. How can you be empathetic and build a loving humane relationship if you already think you know what people should hear? Empathy and love is about questioning yourself about the needs and expectations of the audience. Or even simple, asking your own self, "How do you want people speak to you?" Your voice should have that warmth that leaves people waiting as to when you will turn to them. Be obsessed about making people feel good. Ultimately your speech is not about you; it's about audience. Get into the hall a bit early. Mingle up a little with them before you start your presentation. The best part is that when you mingle up, you forget even about your own nervousness. So get into their boots and focus more on their needs. Give them this crazy amount of value they have possibly never experienced before.

You don't always have to read from the script. Relive your experiences by connecting them to your message. Give them some side details. A teacher gets boring if he sticks to this so called divine script – the syllabus. Sharing experiences by using words of warmth makes your audience feel what you are feeling and that's what empathy and love is all about.

The world is getting too boring and too formal when it comes to dealings between people. Think a little out of box and try to be more human. Let your speech reflect some emotions, happiness and sensitivity. Introducing the elements of love in your speeches makes it fun and excitement and always leaves people wanting more.

Expectations off the Stage: Ever wonder why is there this sudden silence when a particular teacher enters the classroom and why aren't students moved in presence of some other teacher as if he is not there? Of late, I did notice this behavior keenly and found one of the biggest reasons behind the teacher ineffectiveness. Believe me, it is not something you can control in the class. It is something beyond what you do on the stage or inside the classroom. Yes, you probably got me. I am speaking about the activities off the stage. During my communication training sessions with many of my students I noticed how the audience gets serious when they see a particular student coming to the podium. And then there are other buddies who even though try to look more furious than the first one, but couldn't really get the desired attention. A few months observation of this scenario gave me some shocking results. I noticed the students or teachers who are not serious or formal enough in there off stage activities are not taken seriously when they are on the stage. Such speakers rather engage in, what I would call as, some "Value Losing" activities. These are the activities that humans consciously or sub-consciously do not expect from other humans. Even though people may themselves be part of these activities but deep down they realize them being something to avoid. I tried to work on these activities for myself and guess what, the results were astonishing. We will know about some of these activities in this part of our discussion, the purpose being to avoid indulging in any of these; lest your presence on stage becomes weightless.

Negativity: People don't want negativity in their lives, they have had enough. Poverty, harassment, killings, racism and what not, it's in discussion all over from home to office. We really need some break from this. You don't have to be someone who always blames people and system for anything happening around. Optimism is not to be shown at the podium only. A speaker should always be looking for that silver lining among clouds. An effective speaker on stage is a counselor off the stage, and a counselor is filled with positivity and optimism up to his brim. The criticism and negativity may initially seem to be catchy, bringing out the dimensions we never heard of before. But people ultimately lose hope and fall in despair, something they don't want. Accept it or not, if such a speaker gets to the podium, he may find all eyes open but no ear really listening.

Complaining: Meetings or conversations with some people are full of complaints against almost everyone. They don't accept being wrong or having made a mistake. They would storm out or fight till end to prove they are right, even if everyone else points out their mistake. Such speakers are already losing out their influence on people. The audience always wants to listen to someone who looks human and when a mistake happens of him, accepts it with sincere apologies. Remember, complaining is a viral misery. It doesn't lead to sunshine.

Back-Biting: We generally make fun out of gossiping. We like talking about others not even bothering we may be scratching their back. And the person gossiping about others would for the most part gossip about you when you leave his company. A teacher has to be careful about this especially if he shares dinning and recreational facilities with students. A teacher giving in to gossiping or back-biting can never win hearts of his pupil. Make it a habit. Speak well about people at their backs. It opens up the hearts of those listening to you. And if they are the ones who make up your audience, you have an edge.

Exaggeration: Things are to be mentioned as they are. Some people believe in creating embroidery over things. This exaggeration mostly

71

leads to lying and consequently people don't like to listen to someone who is lying to them. Now, there are people who confuse exaggeration and emphasis. While emphasis is giving a word the attention it needs, exaggeration is willful repetition of things making people forcefully believe it.

Dogmatism: As in some kind of sacred text. The dogmatic people believe they are undeniably true. Such people don't even consider what others have to say. They would be dominant in any kind of discussions even without a base to their knowledge. A dogmatic teacher would never entertain a question in his class in the first place. And if he ever does, there is no second guess to his answer. Consequently, people won't even like to attend the classes of such person.

Besides, criticism, self-depreciating attitude and holding on to grudges for too long are some other off stage activities we should be weary about. We simply have to be professionals and humans in our conduct and avoid indulging in anything shaking up our image as a person in general and speaker in particular.

The Timeliness: Speaking the simplest way, people expect you to show up on time and finish in time. Like most of us, speakers find no problem starting on time. It's the second part they get in trouble for – finishing on time. Heard of the phrase, "it's easy to begin, difficult to stop"? Well, that may be true for the most but in public speaking this is something to be checked. Off stage if you are asked for a counsel or a feedback, be brief and within the context. Nobody likes being given a lecture or be talked at. Try to know what people want to hear exactly from you and give them what's desired. If you are known for your endless advices, people won't come to you even if you have something valuable to offer. And then you carry it to the stage as well. On stage, you may find people not leaving the hall during your speech, however, not for the sake of listening or learning. It would just be for the sake of being there, for a compulsive presence. Ask yourself, how many times have you been to academic or non-academic sessions where you never wanted to be by heart, but worry of falling short of attendance or threat of your absence being noticed by management forced you to stay there? I have noticed this keenly in various sessions of formal and informal settings. People are not time conscious. Bet it a key note speaker at a conference, somebody there for a welcome speech, a guy introducing a speaker, a teacher in a class or sometimes the host, they just seem to be going on forever.

During my multi-year teaching experience I have noticed a harsh lag on part of the teachers. Mostly, they won't finish the class on time and won't think of leaving until the next teacher bangs the door. In a typical college or university of Indian settings, a student has to show up for 5 consecutive classes, each lasting for more than an hour with a short lunch break. No matter the teaching methodology used, almost every teacher is broadcasting the content and students have to bear it. Under such settings that can't possibly be changed by teachers, there is something you as a speaker or teacher can do. You can be human, you can be time conscious. If you are asked to speak for 60 minutes, aim for 55 minutes. You audience will love you for that. Ever heard of a complaint from audience that speech was too short? Not likely, right? But about presentations and lectures seemingly going on forever, I have heard plenty of complaints.

A public speaker, especially a teacher needs to be mindful of the fact that he is not there for his own pleasure, but for the pleasure of his audience. People can get up and leave anytime. Mostly, they won't do that, but they have the option.

Winding up our discussion of the hidden expectations, I want my readers to realize that we all have obligations to meet audience expectations – open or hidden. They may not be paying us for that in currency, rather something more valuable than currency – their presence and time.

PRINCIPLE OF COMMUNICATION MIX

One of my friends in Delhi had gone for the interview for some vacancy in American Express. Unfortunately, he was rejected and was given a detailed feedback about his interview performance. Before breaking up his feedback in many bullet points, the company had summed up all feedback in three words in bold just above the break up details. It read, "Ineffective Communication Skills". Well, this got me on my toes and I desperately wanted to know the details. Possibly because I was myself working in service sector and had to keep my options wide open in case I had to switch. I had to know something about communication skills especially the "ineffective" ones. So I started reading through the paper. When I finished reading it, I had a big time shock. Of all the bullet points I didn't find a single point saying something about other than my friend's speech and voice. The complete reading had statements like, "Your voice was not clear so the panel thought our clients would have hard time understanding you", "You speak at an enormous pace and that might not fit for the telephonic conversations with our business associates", "We could notice some mother tongue influence (MTI) in your speech, that would give our clients the feeling of talking to some non-native person and they would be uncomfortable". The complete document had something to say about my friend's speech and the only conclusion I could draw from this feedback was that my friend had not been rejected for "ineffective communications skills", but "ineffective speaking skills". I could see the world in general and the executive who typed this letter in particular is yet to know the difference between 'communication skills' and 'speaking skills'. Speaking skills make up only a part of the communication skills. A person lacking effective speaking skills may not necessarily be a bad communicator and this was proved by "Albert Mahrebain" in his communication model wherein he reported his research results that communication skills other than speaking skills, result in 57% effect on audience. Your message or in this case my friend's answer to every question accounts for only 7% effect and 37% effect is created by the way you deliver your message. The major inference to be drawn from this research is that non-verbal communication accounts for the 57% influence on audience and forms

74

the major part of communication. The notion is common all over, people mistake communication classes for language or speaking classes. However, the fact is that communication is a very broad term and entails the "conduct in life", not just the voice or speech.

In this chapter, we would discuss the ingredients of communication or the activities that come together in a finely crafted way and give rise to the benevolent act of communication. These ingredients which come together are collectively called as "mix". Just as if you have to know and understand the subject of marketing, you would be required to go through the concept of "marketing mix" which is the result of four marketing activities, also called 4Ps – Product, Price, Promotion and place. In the same way, to know about communication we have to understand the components that make it up. We can collectively call the components as "Communication mix" that includes the activities of Gesturing, Listening, Observing, Writing and Speaking. One can remember all five of them in sequence by remembering the word "GLOWS".

In analogy, the speaker glows only if he GLOWS.

Having discussed the "G" of GLOWS already in our previous chapter – The principle of Gestures and Body Language, We would be dealing with LOWS here. Should you ignore the LOWS of communication, it can really bring you low.

L- Listening: Let's start with Robert Cialdini's Principle of Reciprocity, which states that, "human beings are hard-wired to give back to those who have given to them. And perhaps the greatest gift people can give one another is the gift of attention, a gift you give primarily by listening". The best public speakers in the world are the outstanding listeners. They use their power of listening to grab other people's attention in reciprocity. Now, one may wonder how this actually works. The answer lies in the fact that when you listen to some one, he feels understood and respected. And when you give value to humans they have this innate knack to value you back. They become restless for their want of doing something equally good to you. This works well for a speaker, for if he listens to his audience and makes them feel good, the minimum they can do is to listen back effectively.

So, what else can listening do for a speaker or why it is an integral part of communication that needs to be inherent in a speaker's nature? I will try to answer this question through following headings.

- Persuasive: Listening helps the listener understand the perceptions and feelings of speaker. When you listen to your audience, you can understand them. And when you understand them, you can customize your response to match their expectations and hence persuade them to give a patient and desirable hearing to you. Or to keep it simple, listening becomes persuasive by the application of principle of reciprocity.

- Problem Solving: Most of the times we are not in a position to answer people's questions or resolve their problems because we don't have enough details or understanding of the problem. However, the very details we are looking for could be there in the question and all we need to do is to listen to other party. You can be an effective counselor if you ask the right questions to know the client's situation. That however is possible only if you listen to the details from your client.

- State of Mind: A single solution may not work for two different persons with similar problem. The meaning of the problem and the solution thereby lies in the person's state of mind which is evident from the kind of speech or words he delivers. Listening to some one keenly while he speaks allows you to know his state of mind and respond appropriately.

- They Too Have a Say: As pointed out many times in previous chapters, a rational audience wants to be the part of an interaction and dialogue. They want to be spoken with, not spoken at. They have a lot to offer and want somebody to accept it. It could be in the form of feedback, a suggestion or a correction to the name of a person or place you may have pronounced wrong. A speaker needs to realize the importance of bringing audience to action. This can be done by designing your speech structure such that significant portion of time is kept for audience to have their say and contribute to the session.

- Listen More to Know More: There is no better alternative to know somebody's story than listening to the person himself. Apparently, listening to your audience helps you know more about them and draft your content accordingly. Some experts suggest speaking to few prospect members of audience before you can actually frame your speech. This helps you to listen to their expectations and state of mind.

Ever heard of the adage, "We have two ears but only one mouth"? Besides the general meaning people take from it, which is 'we should speak less and listen to more', there is another slightly different but very adorable meaning for public speakers in it, which is that, "Listening can be twice as important as speaking". This meaning seems to be more comprehensive and more practical from the perspective of public speaking. You don't always have to make mistakes during your speech and learn for future. Sometimes you can listen to other speakers and notice the wrong they are doing. You just have to avoid that. As some genius mind said it;

"Life is too short to keep on rectifying your own mistakes, sometimes we need to learn from mistakes other people make"

When you listen to others, you can figure out how people present information and form arguments. You get to know about that slight different way of doing it that could have created more influence. For example, paying attention to how people use gestures on stage to augment their arguments can really give you an idea about how to gesture effectively in your presentations. Listening to other speakers and watching them speak is just like watching your own recorded video where you get to know what went good and what is to be avoided. So, good listening can really help you in public speaking.

Listening Makes You Credible: Listening well to others is a sign of you being curious and interested in others. You become knowledgeable and thoughtful person given to your ability to understand the meaning of what you hear. Consequently, people perceive you as intelligent and perceptive, someone who can be worth listening to. Further, listening to people while they express the thought and experiences that are very important to them reveals you as someone who cares. This gets especially true when you give people your attention only and refrain from passing judgments, opinions and advices. Such listeners are likely to become good friends and mentors to people. Even if they don't want to advice anyone, people will ultimately ask for it.

When you focus on somebody speaking, you will be able to identify not just the words used in question or any problem being explained but the complex meaning behind the words. You will notice the key points and information that sums up the problem in totality. Sometimes the speaker gives you the verbal clues about the important information and the expectations he has from any possible solution. That's all you would require to be in a position to help someone with their problems or with confusions.

Etiquettes of Listening: Effective listening involves paying both physical and mental attention to the speaker's words and actions. Understanding the message as close in meaning as intended by the speaker is the primary goal of listening. This act of listening has its own norms which are to be followed wholeheartedly by the listener, lest the listening act turns into a mere act of hearing. Here are a few etiquettes we all should follow to ensure effective listening:

- Prepare to listen: Get yourself ready for patient listening. Allow speaker to know your readiness from your body language, eye-contact and positive gestures. Turn completely towards the speaker. The negative poses like showing half face or side eyes should be avoided. Give them this feeling that nothing else is going on in your mind and you are there only for speaker.

- Put him at Ease: Avoid all unnecessary disruptions and questions that disturb the speaker while delivering the message. Let him say it in his own words and terminology. Pretend you are enjoying knowing his story or question and that you are desperate to understand him. As a teacher, invite questions anytime throughout the session and let your pupils know you are there to answer their questions and listen to them.

- Remove Distractions: Get rid of everything that may possibly hamper the speaker from opening up or express himself fully. Turn off all electronic gadgets especially the mobile devices well before they start speaking. If the speaker wants to speak to you in private, make sure it is not publicized. You don't want to be a boss like, "Excuse me team, I need to speak to John for 10 minutes". If co-workers or classmates are talking, tell them to be mum or shift to next seat. Make sure not to tap your pen or marker on the desk or podium while they are speaking. Avoid playing with your body parts especially fingers, hair or tapping foot.

- Do Not talk Unnecessarily: As much as possible, a listener should avoid cutting speakers speech in between and help him keep the rhythm. However, it is not prohibited to clear the confusions a listener might have had due to speaker's words. Moreover, a listener should not remain totally passive during longer speeches on part of the speaker. Doing so actually indicates the lack of interest and absence of mind. Care has to be taken however not to make speaker feel bad. When you speak in between to clear a point or know the situation better, it actually works for you, for he perceives it as your attempt to understand.

- Show Some Empathy: The purpose of listening is not to understand the words, but the meaning and emotions behind the words. It is more like getting into speaker's boots and feeling the need for listening properly. Consequently, if we want people to feel the intensity behind our message, we have to feel theirs.

- Don't Give in to Bias: To benefit from speaker's message, we have to drop our perceptual biases. Biasness filters the message content and allows only that part to move through, that appeals to our stand on the issue being discussed. Most likely, we will miss the intention and emotions behind the message if we give in to bias. Moreover, even if we disagree at some point, we should follow the ethics of disagreement and that would be to give the speaker enough time to make his point and then present our viewpoint.

Rounding off our discussion, it all goes back to the Principle of Reciprocity – The better you listen, the more you will be listened to.

O - Observing: I would rather go against some experts who associate observation with all five senses to know about the objects, events, attitudes and phenomenon around us. I would associate it with the 'sense of sight' coupled with 'presence of mind'. While listening is majorly about the abstract concept of understanding people and their thoughts, observing is the physical phenomenon wherein a person notices stuff happening before his eyes and tries to learn from it. It is clearly the use of sense of sight to take learning inputs from the environment and then using the mind to analyze the situation and draw some meaning.

Observation forms the significant part of the communication and goes a long way making you an effective communicator.

Observation is one of the major tools humans use to learn new things in life. Almost all of the behavioral phenomenon like perception, attitude, learning and many others develop in humans in part due to consistent observation of the environment around. Ever wonder, why does a small kid not more than 2 years of age try to take a phone close to ears even though he knows nothing about this device? Well, he has seen you doing it. Why do behavioral psychologists suggest a couple not to argue before a child? Or why do we refrain from being abusive in front of a child? The answer is just similar to the previous one, a child observes all this and if exposed continuously to any of these forbidden acts, he learns it. Most likely, observation has similar consequences in public speaking too. You don't always have to try and create new gestures or new ways of delivering message. You may sometimes watch experts do it and just imitate. I believe;

Effectiveness does not always come by doing effective things all by yourself, it sometimes comes by observing people doing stuff effectively and adopting it.

There was this story I read in "Young Muslim Digest" back in 2008. It has great implications and relevance to our discussion so I would like to share it with you. So there was a married couple, their kid and a grandfather – all living together. The grandfather was around 85 and for the most part, not keeping well with the dinning trend and cleanliness habits of the family. He would often spoil the dinning table due to shivering in his hands while he picks up anything to eat. Fed up with the mess happening every now and then due to this old man, the couple decided to give him a separate table and a wooden bowl that won't break upon falling down. The old man would serve himself on the separate table now and was ignored if he ever needed something different than what he would normally get. One day, while the kid's father was returning from office, he saw the kid playing with the mud. Approaching close, the man asked, "Hey honey, mind telling me what's happening?" What are you doing with the mud? Replying in his soothing innocent voice, the boy said, "Nothing much dad, am making a mud bowl". Mud bowl? What are going to do with this, asked his father. And the boy said something in reply that shook the land below his father's feet. "Dad, when you grow old, you too would require a separate bowl, so I am making it for you. I would give it to you when I reach your age". The author has entitled the story as "The Wooden Bowl" and undoubtedly reflected a great message. While different people come up with different morals from the story, I come up with something that relates it with my discussion – "The Observation". The kid was observing it all and noticing everything happening around. He learned something from his adults and was to his innocent mind, going to apply it.

A public speaker has to act like this kid and observe other speakers while on stage. There is a lot to learn from everything that people do. If you think any move is creating any influence on the audience, grab it. And if it seems to nullify the speaker's effect, abstain from using it. There would also be many things these speakers do and it suits them, but it may not suit you. We are differently capable and differently blessed people, deep voice may create effect for one speaker and for the next it may seem to be hoarse. Someone seeks attention by his clear accent and you being a non-native can't do that. We need to look at the kind of personality, knowledge, experience and audience we have and analyze what suits us and what suits someone else.

Observation as I mentioned before is 'sense of sight and 'presence of mind'. You can't imitate people with eyes closed and mind unconscious. You will have to look at people carefully, notice them, analyze their moves and see what of this goes well with you.

Observation and Audience: The most important and basic skill we can learn if we want to improve our communication and social skills is being able to observe and gather information. You may have great knowledge and effective delivery, but if you don't know what's going on in front of you then you can never have a chance to influence it. An effective speaker doesn't just broadcast content; he observes every movement of his audience and figures out what state they are in. Such speaker can adjust and tailor-make his message to suit that very moment.

When it comes to audience the primary need is to observe their body language and customize your delivery accordingly. It would be embarrassing to keep on raining information if people are yawning or looking down at their mobile phones. In such a situation, you can stop or break the flow of your speech to break the inertia. You can go for an activity or a thought provoking question. The purpose is to bring the lost audience back.

A general rule of thumb to control the audience is to keep them under continuous observation. A speaker must not only work for effective delivery, he should rather consider effective reception. I have noticed speakers especially teachers getting too much involved in message or concept teaching and letting go off the audience. Such speakers see the audience displaying some awkward behavior, but given to the deep involvement in message they kind of can't yet see it. These speakers suffer from **"Inattentional Blindness** – a term coined by '**Arien Mack and Irvin Rock'**, two researchers at MIT in 1992". Inattentional blindness according to them is the failure to notice a fully visible but unexpected object because attention was engaged on another task, event, or object. We all suffer from this kind of blindness at some level, however the efficiency lies in minimizing its impact and keeping alive the sense of sight to take note of every thing happening around.

W-Writing: While we strive for excellence in all aspect of communication, we can benefit by learning the secrets of good writers as well. There is no doubt that a successful speech or presentation begins with a careful word choices and a thoughtful structure. Many established speakers keep this structure as abstract in their mind. However, not all of us are experienced and nor do we remember everything in order. Most of us, especially the beginners get carried away by our enthusiasm and we jumble up the information that results in saying something at the time when it was not meant to be. This chaos in your speech could easily be avoided by giving your speech a structure and penning it down. Every successful speech is written first. It is then edited and re-edited till a speaker finally finds it apt for the occasion.

We define writing as separate component of communication mix and believe that an effective communicator is a creative writer as well. Writing is in itself a way of communicating, however in public speaking we see what influence does it have on our speech and presentation. The mind blowing story ideas or examples strike your mind while designing the speech and if you don't pen them down, you are most likely going to miss them. Writing gives shape and direction to your speech. As much effective and comprehensive your writing, that effective would be the presentation. During my academic career, I have noticed for myself that as much I stick to my speech plan, my speech becomes equally good. And sticking to you plan is possible only either if you have memorized it or you have written it somewhere. As for memory, speakers tend to forget little things that sometimes are detrimental to the message delivery. However, writing every component of your speech and then practicing it regularly overcomes forgetfulness. We can also use content slides as an aid to our memory and be sure that we stick to our speech plan.

To become a better speaker, we have to start writing more effectively and the following techniques shall help becoming the best writer.

Keep Reading: This technique works in analogy to the observation in speaking. If you want to be a better speaker, you will have to observe the expert speakers speaking. In the similar way if you want to be an effective writer you will have to go through the writings of established authors, columnist and other content writers. This helps you develop thoughts and learn different ways of expressing yourself. A speaker should not stick to his comfort zone when it comes to reading. We will have to stretch our mind and read something different to develop different ideas.

Rewrite What you Read: Chose from your favorite reads and rewrite them by your own words. Speakers find problems sharing stories they read from somewhere. They sometimes can't narrate them well and consequently the story loses charm. This thing can be avoided if we comprehend the readings and write them on our own. Rewriting an article in your own words feels like you being the source of the article. And if that's the case, no one can share this story better than you.

Keep a Record: Believe it or not, keeping a record of your own writings helps improve your writing. It is very important to know how you have evolved over time. When you start writing, let your words flow freely, don't censor them. Remember, nothing gets better in the first attempt. It takes thousands of hours of practice and consistency working on raw stuff and carving out something magnificent out of it.

Look for Writing Opportunities: Living in the age of social media and cloud computing, you have enormous avenues to develop yourself into an effective writer. Comment on blogs and posts with enthusiasm. Write some in-depth comments, don't bind yourself by writing something like "thanks for sharing" or "great post". If possible, join some writer's group wherein you get valuable feedback from comparatively established writers or start taking part in writing competitions. It is not about winning, it's about developing the sense of writing.

Write for Hobby: If you are serious about being an effective presenter or published author, then start writing from now. Try writing 1000-1500 words each day and increase this limit as you move on. The moment you think you are done writing, write some more. Make sure you love writing, don't do it out of compulsion.

One day when you look at your masterpiece, you will be surprised to see what you have given to the world. And when it is all because of your own effort; you can certainly present it or speak about it before world like no one else can.

S – Speaking: Among all components of communication mix this one keeps speakers on their toes. Speaking is quite visible. By saying that I don't mean you can see speaker's words, I actually mean this part of communication mix catches everybody's senses and unfortunately this is what people general judge you for. Technically I mean speaking is quiet audible. Not knowing the benefits of non-verbal communication and having never tried different ways of engaging with people other than speaking, the world would certainly evaluate your communication in terms of your speaking. Remember what happened to my friend when he went for an interview?

Even though the enormous research done on the subject proves that speaking is not every thing in communication, there is still something at the ground level that has not changed. The audience in the hall, panel in an interview, students inside the class and the listeners of other types are still driven by the way a person speaks before them. This is where a speaker gets entangled in contemporary practice of ignoring other communication forms and focuses on just speaking. Even if we share the opinion of speaking not being everything in communication, the fact of it being an important component can never be denied. We anyways need to work on it and be effective speakers.

"Speaking is to the communication as head is to the body. To a body, head is not everything. However, remove the head and you know what happens".

We have discussed the effective ways of speaking in terms of pace, tone, pitch and volume in Chapter 5 of this book. Herein we would know why speaking seems to overwhelm whole concept of communication. We would rather try to see what makes speaking so important.

Speaking is Praiseworthy: Your ability to speak is revered by everyone because people fear speaking before audience. You won't always have important things to say, it would just be what other people had to say all along. However, the difference lies in that you as a speaker are not undiscovered. Your speaking would give you the courage to stand out of the crowd, open to new people and new experiences. What brings more praise is that by speaking you become more friendly and approachable, a partner for meaningful conversations and people consider you someone worth sharing ideas with.

A Courageous Task: There is something that happens to people when they face audience. Imagine 100 different faces sitting in a hall, all focusing on you with their diverse experiences and different mind set. And then you have a message which they may not even accept or believe in. If you were an experienced speaker you would somehow manage, but for a beginner it really needs courage and conviction. That's anyways all it takes to make a difference in the world - being able to speak what's in your heart and mind.

Risk of Shame: This is the biggest fear that keeps people away from the podium. What happens if I forget? What if someone asks a question I don't know the answer of? Then, the unthinkable might happen next and everyone would laugh at me. Such thoughts convince people they are better off not going to the stage. However, these questions remain unanswered unless you actually face it. Nothing catapults your speaking ability like working in front of a live audience. When people step in front of the audience, they are taking a huge risk. It is this risk of going live that develops them into a great speaker rather than speaking in front of a bedroom mirror.

More Evident than Non-Verbal Communication: Even though communication starts non-verbally right from the time you show up on the stage, people however start making evaluation only after you start speaking. It is because your message or topic is directly conveyed to them through words and the non-verbal part acts as a supplement. Speaking frankly, non-verbal part is not even needed if your message intensity is strong. People get carried away by your words when you share an emotional message and they won't even notice about hand gestures and body language. However, that's rare. Not every statement you make is emotional or intensified. Non-verbal part is detrimental at times and speaks more than words. Humans have this tendency to give attention to something that demands attention and words demand attention through voice and volume.

Speaking Means Control: The proficiency in all components of communication mix is necessary to become a well-rounded communicator, but the ability to speak well has something different to offer. The capacity to put words together in a way to reflect feelings, thoughts and opinions gives a speaker the advantage of persuading and directing people. Through speaking you get the innate opportunity to make your beliefs and opinions known to the world. You can use your speaking talent to fight for a cause.

Speaking has Power: Mostly, when people think of speaking, they tend to think of it as a common skill. Well, think again. The ability to stand before others and then speaking confidently is not at all an ordinary skill. Read about the triumphs and fall of nations, you would certainly find that speaking has induced and stopped wars. The conflicts start by words and reckless speeches to which others respond in a similar way. When speaking gets intensified, people turn to arms. Speaking has power to change the fate of the world, of the nations, of society and mostly of speaker himself. Your words can tie people together and at the same time break them apart. You can gain excellent reputation through speaking over time, which consequently results in certain credibility to you as a speaker.

In effect, a speaker has to master and be proficient in all five components of the communication mix – GLOWS. All five are to be used as supplement to one another giving your message a definite meaning. We round off our discussion by concluding that effective speaking takes its inputs from other components like Listening, observing and writing. Together all four coupled with gesturing make you an effective communicator.

PRINCIPLE OF DOs and DON'Ts

Having discussed all major dimensions of communication and public speaking, I believe you have developed a fair understanding about being an effective communicator. Now is the time to share some very important tips that I have developed in my role as communications trainer. When you read them, you will certainly find them speaking of common sense. However, not everyone weighs them equally as I do. Possibly because no one thought about them as I did and nobody found them as helping as I did. Give them a careful read and mind them next time you find yourself standing before crowd.

Don't try to be a great Speaker: We are not there to beat any competition and be the best speaker of all. Our sole purpose is to be an effective communicator who can send across his message so nicely that audience feels grateful. We should not keep longing for praise and standing ovations; we should rather show the best of ourselves and try to connect with audience. I believe there is no competition in public speaking, because every speaker has different domain, competencies and natural abilities which nullify the notion of being a great public speaker. Be yourself and do not compare with anyone else. If you ever have to look towards others, let it be for learning purposes – taking what's good in them and ignoring what feels bad.

Let go Off the Public: No, Please don't get me wrong, lest I may be contradicting what we discussed earlier about audience engagement. The audience is really important and your speech in the first place is designed only to appeal to them, not to comfort yourself. When I say 'let go off the public' I mean don't overlook your message and delivery. If you are a beginner, your consideration of audience will make your nervous and less confident. So I suggest let go off them now and focus on your speech.
Ever noticed, that in our daily conversations we have no problem being ourselves? Yet too often when we hit the stage, something changes. The reason is just evident; we focus on audience at the expense of our speaking. When you move across the continuum of speaking you can

easily develop the harmony between your speech and audience, but initially you have to be a little aligned to your message and not the audience.

Don't let mistakes stop you: "To err is human" and even most established speakers make mistakes during their presentation. The strategy to overcome your mistakes lies in the fact that no one notices them in your audience as much as you do. Keep going and don't stop for any minor slip like forgetting a word. This may actually work for you sometimes, because it makes you human and allows you to connect with people. Unless you realize your mistake was really the shaking one, you should not even be apologetic for it. During my communication sessions with number of my students, I have noticed that people generally don't notice the mistakes a speaker makes unless speaker himself stops or gives in to some strange behavior letting people know something has happened. As we say, 'ignorance is bliss' – when it comes to mistakes during your speech, your ignorance of them really turns out to be the bliss.

Speak With a Purpose: Your purpose gives a tone to your speech. So throughout your presentation, think about the reason of you being there. You could be there to teach, entertain, instruct or to motivate. Whatever be the purpose, you have to stick to it and make sure your audience receives what you have to offer. Remember the valuable resource of time they are investing in you, you don't want to hang out with them non-purposefully and leave them lost. Speak of the communication ethics and you would see the purpose ranked on top. It doesn't just help your audience; it makes you feel good throughout. We also call it speaking with intent and it moves people to action. The outcome of your purposeful speech is that people would at least feel different, if not do anything different than they would have before your speech.

Feel Positive About your Session: "What we think about is ultimately what we bring about". I heard this quote in one of the highly inspirational videos "The Secret". To my excitement it has always worked that way for my public speaking and for others whom I tried to know from. Don't ever let negativity drown your confidence, feel good about your speech. Speak to yourself before a mirror every time you are going to hit the stage and say, "This is going to be the best speech I have ever delivered". I was reading an article from IESE Business school published in Forbes in April 2016, they suggest visualizing your speech to the extent that you should see yourself at the end of the speech surrounded by people asking questions, visualize the applause.

Never Exaggerate on Audience Reactions: Someone in your audience is always going to be yawning or playing with their phone, not because of your speech being boring, but their own state of affairs. The guy you see yawning might have had a little sleep last night and the next one you see playing with phone may just be opening the voice recorder on his phone to save your speech for future help. Feels good, right? It is true that audience behavior and body language follows the effectiveness of your speech; however that may not always be the case. You may find people bored and tired because they have been sitting at the same place since last 5 hours and want some break. I have noticed this kind of audience reaction particularly in Indian Colleges and universities where academic curriculum is designed such that students are compelled to sit from 10 Am to 4 PM in one hall, on the same benches to hear out all teachers throughout. In such scenarios, the teacher who comes for the last class is bound to see the lost, tired and bored audience. Irrespective of the fact that you have spent 3 hours preparing this lecture and that you have something great to deliver, you won't find these students receptive enough.

The solution lies in being prepared enough for your session and try to engage your audience as much as possible. After that, if you notice any undesirable reactions, they would have nothing to do with you personally as a speaker.

Acknowledge Yourself for Future: There is no one as strong a critic about your speech as your own self. You are the only one to drag yourself down for a bad speech. You should have pride in your work and recognize any efforts you put towards speaking business. Brain Stacy – a global speaker with speaking experience in 69 countries says, "When you finish a speech or delivering a presentation, give yourself a pat on the back. You overcame your fears and you did it". There may however be times when you are not satisfied with what happened on the stage and you don't feel up. Even then, I believe you should not let yourself down and give in to despair. Have confidence and trust yourself. You can do certainly better. After all this was not the only chance.

Don't Think of Audience as Foes: One of the major reasons that keep people off the stage is the fear that audience won't let them succeed. Primarily, I have noticed this thinking in beginners especially the students of junior semesters. They think people are there to laugh and pull their leg. This however seems to be a pure allegation and doesn't find any base in public speaking. I believe this thinking is the result of lack of confidence and the fear of facing audience. Anyone who believes that audience is anti-speaker should ask himself a question, "Why would someone come to attend your session?" If we are like-minded, the answer would be 'to learn or know something'. Now, if that's the case the audience would like to see the speaker at his best, because if the speaker delivers his best, as audience you have greater chances to learn and know things. So naturally, your audience would like you to succeed and do well. People are very rational when it comes to investing time. And about formal sessions of public speaking, there is no way they can act as your foes and waste their own time.

Connect, Don't Broadcast: People don't come to your sessions just to hear you out. Formally or informally, that's what they have been doing all day. Give them something different – connect with them. An easy way to do this would be to inculcate emotions like happiness, anger, sadness, fear and surprise in your message. People connect to any of these emotions and can relate to your message. As a speaker, don't make your statement look like an argument. Doing so makes us look egotistical. We should rather make a point or tell a story. We can use authentic stories from our own life. People love to know about our passion, life and the things we truly and really care about.

Avoid Being Inappropriate: It would always be a bad idea to poke fun at somebody's religion, race, gender or ethnicity. When addressing a crowd, we have to be adults and look very much rational. Avoid using any sort of cursing or divisive language that may get you in trouble afterwards. As a public speaker people know you are frank and may be liberal in thinking, however sexually suggestive language is to be kept to your inner thoughts.
It may work for a renowned speaker like 'Gary Vaynerchuk' possibly because his expertise outshines his occasional inappropriate language. Genuinely however, we bind our options of traveling Far East or Muslim nations with this speaking attitude. We have to be appropriate enough so that all age groups and mixed gender can make up our audience and feel proud being there.

Never Say You Are Nervous: Public speaking is not an easy job; people are as scared of facing the audience as they are of death. As Mark Twain once said, "There are two types of speakers in the world, those who are nervous and those who are liars". By calling the second group liars, he meant that even they are nervous; they just want to hide it. So they are lying. Even the people of highest profile who have addressed millions of people find themselves nervous. The only difference is that their confidence which is the result of their years of experience hides their nervousness well. One of the biggest mistakes you could do on the stage is to disclose that you are nervous. People can't always read you and they would never know you are nervous. But clueing your audience about it will not make them think any good of your speech.

By telling them you are nervous, you are giving them glasses through which they see you now. These are the "Nervousness Glasses" and anything you say or do afterwards would be checked for nervousness first. Don't disclose it, let it be a secret. Put your confidence on full display instead. If you are confident, people perceive you to be competent, accurate, intelligent, knowledgeable and believable.

Try Speaking Extemporaneously: Don't try to memorize your speeches especially if you are speaking for more than 10 minutes; your memory may betray you by causing you to fumble over a section if you don't say it right. You don't want to look robotic, forgetting the emotions and intensity behind your message. Progress naturally through your speech instead and try to have a free conversation with people. If your speech is long and you fear you might go off the track or forget an important point, it's better to go with extemporaneous speaking style. Here you note down the heading and sub-headings on a piece of paper or take away slides. They only act as a supplement to your memory and keep you within the limits of your speech design. The speech supplements don't have to be detailed and you should only turn to them when needed.

Extemporaneous speaking needs enough practice. You need to understand every detail that underlies a particular heading. People are often seen planning for extemporaneous speech but end up delivering a manuscript speech – the speech type you see your country's foreign minister, Prime minister or president delivering at United Nations General Assembly or country's parliament houses. In such speeches, people often turn to their supplements and make little eye contact with audience. It may work for politicians at UNGA or parliaments, because everything they say is a high-stake matter of foreign policy and they don't want to miss a single word. But for us as academicians, motivators, entertainers and public speakers, manuscript speech is not an option. Our effectiveness lies in connecting with people, engaging and interacting with them. For that we need to go extemporaneously.

Choose Your Own Way: You may find great deal of advice regarding communication and public speaking both online and in print like this book. All authors and experts suggest the techniques and ways that they believe work fine. However all of these suggestions should work as inputs to craft your own strategies. We are all different, and our differences are evident from the physical, mental and social traits we possess. Our voice qualities differ, so does our knowledge and cultural background. We gesture differently and don't speak the same language. Given to our different religious and social background, our understanding of time and space in communication varies a great deal. In that sense, what works for an American or English expert in the west may not work for you in India. Try to act local or native and be yourself in front of the people. Failing to do that makes people view your speech as insincere and calculated, no matter how well you have rehearsed and how much you believe in your message.

Consider the SSA (Speaker, Subject and Audience) principle that we discussed in the first chapter of this book and craft your presentation strategies accordingly. You will find yourself in good shape as long as you prepare well and try to look confident.

Display Some Energy and Enthusiasm: You have to be excited about your topic and that should reflect from your body language and the way you deliver your words. There is no way you can expect your audience to be excited, if you are not excited on your own. Excitement doesn't mean jumping in joy and kicking the floor with energy, nor is it speaking in unnatural raised voice that creates more of a noise than any effect on people. The raised voice and waving arms are to be avoided. Enthusiasm is all about using positive body language, adopting confident postures and speaking clearly with varying intensity and emphasis on words. One golden rule to follow to generate automatic energy in your speech is to prepare well and gain control on your content. Put it rather differently, energy follows confidence.

Label your anxiety as excitement; you will end up feeling more comfortable. Further, the feeling of excitement will shine through any nervousness you may have during your presentation. If you want people be moved by your presentation, bring some passion and a level of sincerity in your emotions while communicating.

Don't be Choosy in Eye Contact: A speaker should not let proximity rule his delivery. Everyone has come to listen to you, whether they sit next to the speaker or in the last row near the exit. All of them demand equal attention and interaction. Bring to your mind the sessions you have attended in the past, how many times did you find a speaker ending up interacting with the front row or a particular group sitting nearby? I have seen enough of them, and I believe you have also been through these boring sessions where you find yourself being ignored for a group. It might as well have worked in reverse where you found yourself to be the center of attention, as if the speaker came for you only. Such speakers act as if there is no one else besides this group and they are bound to lose the audience as they move on. You have to be careful about not getting carried away by the response or nod a particular group gives you. You have to maintain uniform eye contact through the hall and keep everyone engaged.

Avoid Using Fillers in Your Speech: I would rather suggest taking pauses in your speech and think in your mind than using the words like Aaa…, Umm… as fillers. These fillers give your audience the notion that you are thinking and have not prepared your presentation enough. Taking pauses leaves your audience anticipating as to what's coming next and they perceive it to be something important.

Some speakers use what I call as "Pet Words" as fillers and would keep on repeating them every time they finish a sentence or a thought. I once happened to count a speaker's pet word usage in his speech and to my shock he used "You know what I am saying" 8 times in just 2 minutes. The common pet words I have found speakers using as fillers in their speech are - Right…, You know…, Okay?, Getting me?...Understand me?, Fine, Alright.

The reason of using these words in public speaking is that these speakers use them in their daily routine. So, before you hit the stage you would be required to analyze your normal speech pattern and see if there is any pet word that needs to be removed. It gets hard to even recognize the pet word we use in our routine conversations because this has to do with the sub-conscious mind and it doesn't catch your attention often.

A general rule of thumb will be to speak before a friend or a family member and tell them to figure out any such word in your speech that's being repeated.

Avoid Jargons and Technical Words: You could be very well versed with technical knowledge of your subject and may have developed your own jargons and terminology for convenience. However, people are not equally proficient in your subject. If they were, they won't be sitting before you in the first place. Try to use common language and familiar words that are comprehended by every one. Should you find yourself in a situation where you have to use some jargon or technical word, make sure you tell them what it means literally and what is its usage here.

I once happened to chat with an African American customer at my job. When I explained the terms and conditions of our business association, I confirmed if he understood them well. He wrote the word "Gotcha". I went dumb for a while figuring out what gotcha meant. Realizing the dead air in my interaction I took a leap of faith and said, "thank you, what else can I do for you?" Later, I went to Google to confirm what Gotcha meant. I was happy to have hit it right; Gotcha meant "I got you" and they pronounce it as "Gotch-Ye". Truly, this is what jargons and technical words can do to your audience. They may just not hit it right and feel lost in complexity you have bestowed upon them.

Give them readily comprehensible words and don't drive them to too much of thinking, lest they lose the very essence of your message.

Less Is Usually More: If you have been allotted 60 minutes for a speech, don't try to fill this entire time given to you. Surprise your audience by finishing a little early and leave them wanting more. You can use the remaining time for questions your audience may have. And if that's not the case, letting them out a little earlier is not the bad option either. Getting your point across may not always require you to use the allotted time fully, keep it short and sweet and say only what you need to say.

As said by Richard Zeoli, "It is better to leave your listeners wishing that you had spoken for just a few more minutes than squirming in their sweats waiting for your speech to finally end". To see this happening, make sure you keep your presentation just a bit shorter than anticipated.

Be a Storyteller: There are thousands of TED talks we all have been through. Take a look at the ones that have been viewed and liked the most, you will find one thing common in all of them – they are extremely story driven. And this is what in part makes them so popular and inspirational. You can use classical stories or stories of your own experiences to bring context to your speech.

Quoting Peter Khoury in his article, "Characteristics of Effective Public Speakers", "The best presentations don't feel like presentations, they are simply stories told by people with interesting experiences". Storytelling if handled well, could be a powerful tool that doesn't just help in effective delivery, it make sure that people retain the information as well.

Now, if you have really understood everything that we discussed so far about starting off the presentation and then taking it forward with zeal and energy, there is one last but very important thing you need to know before you actually hit the stage. And that's "How to wind up?" You don't want to spoil anything or everything at last, so as a speaker you have to know something about the effective conclusion. To this end, we dedicate the last chapter of our book to understand the 'Principle of Conclusion'.

PRINCIPLE OF CONCLUSION

The concept of recency has its influence on every interaction we have with people just as primacy that we discussed in first chapter. While finishing our conversation, what we say at last has lasting impact on our listeners. Imagine your long term relationship or association with someone that came to an end a while ago. When you go through their memories, what is it that comes to your mind the most? An average person doesn't and can't remember everything that happened in this relationship. Given to the normal thinking patterns he remembers only a few occasions that either make him smile or haunt him. The two important occasions that you possibly never forget about a relationship are 'how it all started' and 'how it came to an end'. And in between, everything is not important. Now in analogy, the public speaking works the same way. Your audience may not remember every minute detail you shared with them; however what they are certainly going to remember is how you started off and how you ended your interaction with them. We won't speak about taking off here, that part has been fairly discussed under the Principle of Introduction. We will discuss the successful and convenient landing here. After all, we believe that 'All is well that ends well'.

Doesn't matter how effective you have been through your speech, if you don't know how to conclude, your key points may get lost and the standing ovation you wanted would be still a dream. So to make sure your speech ends powerfully, try incorporating the following in your speech conclusion.

Summarize Your Message: If you are a beginner and have no idea about ending a speech, here is the breather for you. You can follow the simple formula for any talk which involves three steps.
- Say what you are going to say.
- Say it.
- Then, say what you just said.

You can simply begin your conclusion by saying, "Let me summarize the main points" and then list the key points showing how each of them is related to other points. You can end the summary of the key points by either using a powerful quotation or throwing a challenge at your audience. However, to know whether to use a quotation or a challenge to end your speech, ask yourself what you want people to feel or do after listening to this conclusion. Put it rather simple; try to know the purpose of your speech.

If for example, you have summarized the key points of your speech, the purpose of which is to inspire people or motivate them to work towards the fulfillment of their dreams, you can use the following quote to propel people into action.

"In his international bestseller 'You Can Win', Shiv Khera says, *'Dreams are not those that you see while sleeping. Dreams are those that don't let you sleep.'* Now is the time to introspect and ask yourself, 'do your dreams take you to sleep or they don't let you sleep?"

The other way to conclude with a bang is to summarize your message and throw a challenge at your audience. To tell you how this works, let me share with you the story of one of my own seminars I organized a while ago. I was speaking to motivate my students about writing an effective covering letter. After speaking for almost 40 minutes about the structure, content and importance of the covering letter, I reiterated the main points and reached my closing sentence which was like this:

"The big guns of corporate out there are waiting for you. All they want to see is what is good about you and how can your talent and skills help them with their problems. All they need is to go through your self-speaking covering letter. It takes just one effective covering letter to land in your dream job. Can you design it? Will you write it? Your parents would be happy and you will cherish it. Go for it!"

Finish With a Story: I have seen many inspirational talks ending with a story that illustrated what speaker was talking about. These are the stories with moral that goes exactly with the key message of your speech. While you narrate the story to the people, tell them what the moral of the story is and don't leave them guessing about it. Should you not tell them what the moral is, they may not be able to relate the story to your message.

In one of my sessions about Time Management, I particularly spoke about "Setting Priorities - Doing the right thing at the right time". After finishing all the talking I said, *"Let me share a story with you that will give a fair idea about priorities – doing things when they should be done"*. And the Story went like this:

There were two friends in Delhi who wanted to be civil servants and had joined a coaching academy to qualify India's top civil services examination – IAS (Indian Administrative Services). One of them (Mudasir) had already attempted to qualify the examination a year ago, but couldn't make it. He was living in Delhi since 15 months when the next guy (Shahnaz) joined him. As per routine they would study till 1:00 AM in the night and then go for a walk in nearby streets to freshen up for more studies. One Cold night in January, they set out for a walk and passed by a house where they saw a night watchman at the gate. He must have been in his late 60s and was shivering with cold. He had collected some wood and papers and set them ablaze to get some warmth. Noticing the watchman's dismay, Shahnaz said, "Look at the irony, the owner and his family must be enjoying in warm and cozy mattresses, and this old man, he is dying of cold". To this Mudasir, who was there since months and had known the neighborhood well, replied, "Do you know what; this is SSP's (Senior Superintendent of Police – a white collar rank in Indian Police Services) house. And whatever the SSP and the watchman are doing right now is the result of their own priorities and choices. It's because of what they chose to do with their time". Shahnaz, not getting his senior friend well, asked, "What do you mean?" To this Mudasir replied and said something that I want you all to listen carefully. He said, "Go back 30 years from now, you will certainly find SSP awake at this time of the night, studying and burning the midnight fuel. You will find him doing something he was supposed to do then, the right thing. Now look at the watchman, you will find him enjoying in his kind of cozy and warm mattress. He didn't do what he was supposed to. Under normal circumstances, both of them must have had a choice either to bear the sleepless nights or enjoy the sleeping. The SSP chose the sleepless nights and watchman the otherwise. Now is the time, SSP will enjoy sleeping forever and the watchman will have to bear the sleepless nights. It's all about setting priorities in your life and doing the right thing at the right time."

After I finished the story, I said, "Now ask yourself, what are your priorities and what do you want to do with your time?" Guess what, my audience had to stand and put their hands together. My conclusion worked well with a story, so could be yours.

Call Them to Action: If your talk is of a persuasive kind, the closing statement you make is referred to as call to action. So if you are trying to persuade your audience to take action, you should end by telling them what exactly you want them to do. The words you use to call them to action are the most memorable and in essence, the main takeaways for your audience. Your call to action is something you want your listeners to remember even if they forget everything else in the speech.

For instance, if your speech was meant to persuade people about blood donation, your call to action would be a strong request urging them to consider blood donation. You could end by saying, *"While you all believe in giving something back to the society, please consider giving blood, you could save a life"*. Quoting Brain Tracy, "when you are delivering a call to action, pick up your energy and tempo. Speak with strength and emphasis. Regardless of whether the audience participants agree with you or are willing to do what you ask, it should be perfectly clear to them what you are requesting."

End with Humor: If you have been using humor throughout your speech and you think it's appropriate to the kind of audience and message, there is no harm winding up your speech with humor. We always like to feel good. So if you conclude by leaving people laughing and smiling, how can that be a bad thing?

Occasionally, I believe you can try using the title of your speech to close and this can have dramatic effect on people listening. For instance, if your speech is a kind of inspiration where you start by asking people a question "What's holding you back?" You can go through your talk effectively and end by saying this, *"So let me end this session by asking you the similar question I started with, "What's holding you back"?*

Further, some speakers tie the speech closing to their opening. In this scenario you may start with a story and leave it half way. And then finish the story at speech ending. You may say for example, *"Remember Hafsa I told you about at the beginning of my talk, the one who felt so dumb on the stage that she broke into tears when she tried speaking for the first time? Well, let me update you on her current status. She followed the same principles of communication that I discussed before you, working on them one by one until she mastered them all. Today she is the chief host of all the major events at her university auditorium where she entertains thousands at once"*.

I want to end this part by quoting Fred Miller, a renowned speaking coach, when he says, "Your closing must be strong and compelling. You're going for a 'Knock Out!' It is what the audience will probably remember most, and it's certainly your last opportunity to make a lasting impression".

How Not to End Your Speech:

While we discussed some interesting and effective ways to end our speech, there is also immense need to know of the things we should avoid at conclusion. All the discussion that follows is primarily the result of not planning your speech especially the conclusion well. The old saying "Failing to plan is planning to fail" is aptly described in the following discussion. Try to avoid all these mistakes in your speech endings.

1. Miss-timing the Speech: Many speakers who don't plan their speech well lose the track of their structure. They would take enough time speaking about a thing and not leave any time for something else that was important. Such speakers design a nice conclusion but don't get anytime to present it. This is primarily because they exaggerate too much on the points they think are important and lose the track of the time. An easy way to overcome this problem is to stick to your speech structure and give each component as much time as planned.

2. Going without Conclusion: Some speakers don't plan any conclusion at all and believe in effective delivery of the content only. They are most likely to surprise the audience by ending unexpectedly. An effective speech demands that there is no confusion or ambiguity in the mind of your audience and that they should know this is the end. A speaker literally has to prepare his audience for the end. We generally see such speakers end with something like, "That's all" or "I believe that shall do it", which is not the good idea because it is not the authoritative ending. With this type of ending, your influence and credibility stands detracted.

3. An Apologetic Ending: Should you prefer undermining your credibility as a speaker, this is the best way to achieve this. Speak with confidence and believe that everything has gone well. As suggested earlier, you should never apologize for something minor; the audience usually doesn't notice the mistakes unless you apologize for it. And then there are some speakers who would do everything very nicely but still end like this:
"I apologize for going so long. I know it could be boring listening to someone like me".

4. A Different Tonology: Depending upon the feelings that you want to induce in your audience, a message needs to have a particular tone. If your purpose was to induce some energy and excitement in people and you have used voice-up tone throughout, make sure your ending bears the similar tone as well. Conversely, if you have been emotional and thought provoking throughout your session, the ending doesn't have to be fun and happiness.

5. Speaking after Conclusion: The conclusion is supposed to be the last part of your speech and now your audience prepares to wind up. When you have quoted the saying of a renowned thinker or thrown a concluding challenge at your audience, let them stand up for an ovation and enjoy the moment. Don't speak after you have concluded. Doing so would only create confusion among your audience.

6. Dragging the Conclusion: The introduction and conclusion parts of the speech are supposed to be comparatively shorter than the body. The conclusion of your speech should not look like a discussion. It is supposed to be short and summarized version of your discussion part. Some speakers would say it nicely that, *"In the end, I will tell you a story that would clear the air around our discussion"*. However, when they speak about the moral of the story and try to connect it to their message purpose, they speak longer than the story itself. Resist the temptation to keep going. Cut your conclusion short and let your audience grasp it. In terms of statistics I would go with Lisa B. Marshal, she says, "Your conclusion should be about 10-15% of the entire talk. So if your talk is 15 minutes, then your conclusion should be about 2 minutes. For a 40-minute talk it should be about 4 minutes".

Etiquettes of Conclusion:

If everything that we discussed so far has went as planned for our speech, there are just a few more lines I want to take you through to make sure you leave with a bang. I believe as fellow speakers you should know something that I call as etiquettes of conclusion.

1. Make it clear that you are done. You can do this by saying thank you and moving a step back.
2. While you say thank you, select a few friendly faces among the audience and pass on a smile to them.

3. When you are done and have taken a step back, stand still at that position and do not move forward, backward or sideways.
4. While your audience is clapping, keep looking at them and thank them for applaud. Do not look at the microphone or shuffle papers.
5. When someone starts to applaud or stands up, look at that person with smile and thank him. The rest will know you have ended and will join him.
6. If you have finished your concluding remarks and you see few seconds of silence, don't feel uneasy by this silence. Your audience may just be unsure whether you have finished and may be processing your final remarks. Not to mention, these few seconds may feel like few minutes. However, as a speaker stand there comfortably.
7. Your introducer may come back to the stage to thank you on behalf of your audience. Smile and thank him back. Shake hands warmly.
8. Wave at your audience in a friendly way and then move aside to let introducer or host to take the stage.
9. It is not at all bad to shake hands with few audience members who have been sitting close to you. Quoting Brain Tracy, when you shake hands with one person in the audience, many other people in the audience feel that you are shaking their hands and congratulating them as well.
10. Avoid turning your back to the audience as much as possible and leave the stage with smile.

Besides, there would be many other things that would work for you at conclusion. I may not have spoken about them possibly because I never faced a situation where I could use them. Or it might as well be possible that they never crossed my mind. The etiquettes I mentioned work for me every time I leave the stage and I have read and seen many speaking experts doing the same. However, I believe if there is anything that speaker should be worried about at conclusion, it is 'what makes him feel good and what he thinks makes his audience feel that way'.

The Last Word: Now that I want to finish this discussion and leave you for the best, I want you to know that communication and public speaking is not the alien stuff. It's relevant to me, you and everyone out there in the world. It is something inherent to us as humans that has evolved us over centuries and taken us to where we are today. We are going to need it to evolve further from here. There is no getting away, we all will be part of this evolution and we need to contribute. We all need to know the communication basics, because communication is not just about the podium and stage, it's about everything in our life – it's about our "conduct". Be it your office, college, market, home or playground, communication is about knowing what makes your fellow humans feel valued and then delivering that value.

Dear esteemed reader, I want you to know that communication is not just conveying your message and speaking your mind. It's about emotions and connection that you develop while you interact. You have to tell people your stories and in turn listen to theirs; this is how you take down the barriers in humanity. You have ideas, innovative thoughts, reformist thinking and much more to offer to this world. Nobody is averse to what you have to say, they just want you to say it. Your mind is on boil and you want to speak up for good like Tolerance, Abundance, Love, Relationships, Humanity, Hope, Faith, Gender equality, Motivation, Self-help, Peace and have a say against, discrimination, war, poverty, sexual abuse, harassment, bullying, nationalism, occupation, mass killings, terrorism, corruption and domestic violence. I believe there would certainly be something, if not everything on your mind that can help make this world a better place. But the world has to know this, you need to speak up.

My purpose of writing this book is not just to help you speak before a crowd; rather it is to turn you into someone who people long for. Someone who inspires and finds respect wherever he speaks. The principles discussed herein are universal and find application everywhere whether you speak to two persons or two thousand, in train or an auditorium, in class or corridor, in person or in public. I believe these are not just the principles of communication, they are principles of humanism.

There are numerous sources available globally when it comes to reading about communication and public speaking. However, this book was meant for you to relate to these principles and adopt them in your social

103

and professional life, not just read them. And possibly, that's the reason of keeping the chapters short and precise, discussing only 'How to" aspect of problems we normally face while communicating. Every technique and strategy I have discussed is tested; I have used them for myself over years and tried to share them with everyone who I think needs them. In this book I have just tried to give them a name. Happy for me, I find many renowned global speakers believe in similar techniques and principles.

I will take your leave with these words. We get lot of fun and feel energized listening to inspirational thoughts and reading self help books like this. And about speaking in public, it is a subject that many of us, literally, get excited just thinking about. That ain't any bad. But hold on, think about it for a while. How long have we been doing that? I mean just reading and listening to the stuff and feeling good about it? Isn't now the time to change and follow all the good we read and listen? Is this book going to be just another read for you? What 's going to change if all that you do is be excited or may be talk about this book and not take any action?

Honestly, that's not why I wrote this book. I won't be happy having you go cover to cover on this book and not try any of it in your professional life. No matter your level of communication, try these principles, the change is guaranteed.

I wish you luck with everything good you are into. God be with you all…….. Peace!

Yours Effectively
Mohammad Roomi Rather

www.ingramcontent.com/pod-product-compliance
Lightning Source LLC
Chambersburg PA
CBHW032046040426
42449CB00007B/1005